Through the Storms

Help from Heaven When All Hell Breaks Loose

Tony Cooke

Harrison House
Tulsa, OK

16 15 14 13   10 9 8 7 6 5 4 3 2 1

Through the Storms: Help from Heaven When All Hell Breaks Loose
ISBN: 978-160683-745-0

Published by Harrison House Publishers

Contents

Foreword 9

Introduction 13

Chapter One — Can't I Just Have a Trouble-Free Life? 19

Chapter Two — Jonah's Storm 31

Chapter Three — The Disciples' Storm 43

Chapter Four — Paul's Storm 57

Chapter Five — The Storms Within 67

Chapter Six — It's About the Destination 79

Chapter Seven — The Four-Wheel Drive Christian 89

Chapter Eight — Can I Avoid at Least Some Problems? 103

Chapter Nine — Becoming a Storm Chaser 115

Chapter Ten — Suffering and the Will of God 129

Appendix — Scriptures for the Storms 149

O you afflicted one,
Tossed with tempest, and not comforted,
Behold, I will lay your stones with colorful gems,
And lay your foundations with sapphires.

Isaiah 54:11

For the persecuted Church, whose faith has inspired us all.

This world is not worthy of you.

Foreword

I can honestly say that very few books have ministered to me and touched my heart as much as Tony's latest book, *Through the Storms: Help from Heaven When All Hell Breaks Loose.* Having gone through the diagnosis of cancer, which was the storm of my life, I can relate to all the gems of truth and relevance found between the pages of this book. Tony has amazingly brought a much-needed balance to the subject. He has brought light and truth to those who are in darkness and may be confused. He has masterfully used quotations, illustrations, and scriptures to show us how to navigate through the tough times when storms hit. Everything in this book is applicable—whether someone uses this book as a manual for preparedness before the storm or for what to do during the storm or for how to deal with the aftermath of a storm.

I personally love the chapter on storm chasers. So many people don't know what to do, what to say, or how to help when those close to them are going through storms. Tony gives good advice and counsel on what we can do. I love his honest advice on how we should not try to sound like an expert but instead should allow Scripture to give balance, while also accepting that the unexplainable things are sometimes mysteries of God. Like Tony, I am an optimist, not a fatalist. I had to be that way to survive and overcome my affliction.

All I know is that just as this book, the Bible, and the life I've lived attest, the end of a storm brings rainbows, freshness, growth, and more good than anyone can imagine. This might be hard to believe when the storm looks like it is never going to end, but at the end, it's almost as though it never happened because the blessing far exceeds the storm. Tony's simple yet powerful message proves that every storm has a beginning and an end—whether it was Jonah's storm, the disciples' storm, or Paul's. This is an amazing truth.

Diego Mesa
Senior Pastor of Abundant Living Family Church,
Rancho Cucamonga, California

All of us encounter the storms of life. In this book, Tony Cooke gives some much-needed advice and godly counsel on how we can walk through the storms of life in a successful, God-honoring way. Tony's knowledge and understanding of God's Word shared in this book will enable readers to apply the scriptures to their lives, which will equip them to be ready for the storms they will encounter in the future or are encountering at the present time. Tony's deep desire to help people fulfill their God-given purpose is woven through the pages of this book. This book would have been very helpful to my wife and I when we went through a very difficult storm in our lives—the death of our sixteen-month-old son. This is a must-read for everyone.

Sam Smucker
Senior Pastor of The Worship Center,
Lancaster, Pennsylvania

All of us go through storms in this life, and whether we like it or not, we will have to face them! There are many different kinds of storms, and there are many different reasons why these storms come. A storm in itself can never destroy a child of God, but *how* we face the storms can either make us or break us. Facing our storms with faith in God makes us stronger and better people; living through the storms in dread and in fear can do great damage to our faith.

This is a very special book in many ways. Tony Cooke goes into depth on a subject that many people have a multitude of questions about, offering interesting details and telling us what Scripture actually teaches about the storms of life and suffering so that we can understand the why's and the how's of what we are facing. Then he gives us very practical advice from Scripture on how we can overcome the storms of life. The most fascinating thing about this book is that it also helps impart a kind of maturity into the life of the reader by helping him to understand these things by seeing them as God sees them. So in every way, this is a most practical book!

I faced a huge storm at an early stage in my Christian life. Three days after I came out of Islam to faith in Jesus Christ, God called me to preach the Gospel so I began to share Jesus with others. For this I was confined in a mental institution, was tortured, and spent almost a year in prison. Upon my release, I was told that if I did not renounce Christ and turn back to Islam, I would be executed. By this time I had lost everything that I owned. With seventy-five cents in my pocket, I escaped and left my country as a refugee. It was a very difficult time, but I made it through because of our Heavenly Father's faithfulness and love. God did not take away the storm, but He was with me and walked me through it!

This is truly one of those "must-read" books. This very practical and easy to understand book will help readers in their own storm, and it will also equip them to help others who are going through difficult times in their own lives.

Rev. Christopher Alam
Missionary-Evangelist,
Founder and President of Dynamis World Ministries

Introduction

This really isn't a book about the weather; it's about our lives.

A "storm" is an oft-used metaphor that describes the challenging, difficult seasons of life. When people relate that they're going through a stormy time, we know what they mean. They're telling us that they're facing a period of increased adversity, challenges, and difficulties.

We know that people try to protect themselves from *natural* storms and take precautions in order to make it through safely. People in southern coastal areas are instructed to board up their windows and evacuate when a hurricane is approaching. Folks in tornado alley know about sirens and storm shelters. Those facing a blizzard recognize the importance of snow shovels, snow blowers, and plows. But what wisdom do we have to prepare us for facing the storms of life? Do we know where storms come from? Do we realize that all storms are not the same? Do we realize that the solution for one storm may not be equally helpful when trying to weather a different type of storm? This book provides answers to these questions.

This book also makes it clear that storms come to everyone. One of the ancients said that "man is born to trouble" (Job 5:7). It's true that we live in a fallen, hostile world, and while the Bible gives great hope and strength to believers, it offers no unrealistic picture of utopia in the here-and-now.

> **In the last days there will be very difficult times. For people will love only themselves and their money. They will be boastful and proud, scoffing at God, disobedient to their parents, and ungrateful. They will consider nothing sacred. They will be unloving and unforgiving; they will slander others and have**

> **no self-control. They will be cruel and hate what is good. They will betray their friends, be reckless, be puffed up with pride, and love pleasure rather than God. They will act religious, but they will reject the power that could make them godly. Stay away from people like that!**
>
> **2 Timothy 3:1-5 (NLT)**

Even Jesus spoke of the distress that we would encounter in this world: "...And on the earth distress of nations, with perplexity, the sea and the waves roaring; men's hearts failing them from fear and the expectation of those things which are coming on the earth..." (Luke 21:25-26). Jesus was not a defeatist; instead, He went on to say, "Now when these things begin to happen, look up and lift up your heads, because your redemption draws near" (Luke 21:28).

This is not a fatalistic book. If you're looking for doom and gloom, you're going to have to go elsewhere. What you'll find here is hope. We are looking to a merciful and forgiving God, a God of wisdom and power. A God who has promised to never leave us or forsake us. A God who has promised to see us through.

These are not days for believers to be weakened through dismay or paralyzed by fear. We are to look up with confidence and positive expectation, not look down in despair and hopelessness. Helen Keller had it right when she said, "Although the world is full of suffering, it is also full of the overcoming of it." Instead of being overwhelmed with the pressures of life, we are to lift up our heads in the knowledge that we have a Savior and Deliverer.

This book doesn't offer quick fixes, but the lessons in this book are designed to give you wisdom on how to pass through and move beyond the storms of life. You will learn that God is your ally, not your adversary. You will also discover that God has established clear principles and strategies on how to not just survive but to thrive in the midst of life's challenges.

Diego Mesa knows about storms. Incredibly disciplined, he was the picture of health, having run four marathons in the year prior to being diagnosed with Stage IV kidney cancer in June 2008. His doctor told him he had a 50% chance of living twelve months, but that his condition was so severe he could die any day. Subsequent prognoses were also grim. The consensus of all medical opinion was that this was a death sentence.

Diego cooperated with his doctors and went through conventional treatments, but at the same time he equally and aggressively attacked the cancer by faith, reading Scripture, praying, and seeking God. Diego also tackled his condition through natural regimens involving diet and exercise.

Healing did not come overnight; it was a process. Diego had to fight weariness, discouragement, and fear. When he was first diagnosed, Diego called his friend Pastor Jim Cobrae, who told him, "Diego, we're going to kick the devil's...." I'll leave the rest of that sentence to your imagination, but Jim's statement encouraged Diego to fight the cancer with every fiber of his being. Diego began applying the same disciplines he had used in running marathons. He decided that excuses, compromise, pity parties, and days off were not an option. Diego realized that his faith was not perfect, and at times prayed, "Lord, I believe; help my unbelief!" (Mark 9:24). He knew that Jesus never demanded perfect faith, but said that even faith as small as a mustard seed could move mountains (Matthew 17:20). To this day, my friend Diego continues to pastor a thriving church in southern California.

Sam and Sherlyn Smucker also know about storms. When they were young parents, their sixteen-month-old son Christopher died in a car accident. As they reeled in the confusion and pain of that tragic event, several people offered "answers." A well-meaning relative told them, "God needed another flower in heaven, so He just decided to come and take your little boy." Another said, "God knew your son wouldn't turn out well, so He just took him now." Yet another chided them, saying, "You weren't watching him correctly, and that's why he got out in the road." Fortunately, most people just gave them a hug or put a loving hand on their shoulder and didn't try to explain anything.

Around the time of the funeral, Sam said to Sherlyn, "We do not understand why this happened, but one thing we are going to do is worship God." The decision to worship the Lord kept them from a deep grief and brought an unusual comfort. They knew that God did not take Christopher, and they wanted to glorify the Lord by making the decision to trust Him, depending upon His supernatural ability to bring strength and comfort. Their thought was, "If the enemy is trying to defeat us, he is the one who will be defeated."

Sam prayed, "Lord, if you ever want to show me anything about why this happened, that's fine. If not, that's alright too." Together, the Smuckers decided to serve God in spite of what happened and live their lives to the fullest. Sam and Sherlyn went on to minister graciously and compassionately to countless others and have served as the pastors of The Worship Center in Lancaster, Pennsylvania, for more than three decades.

Christopher Alam is yet another person who knows about storms. Born in a Muslim family with Middle-Eastern origins, Christopher received Jesus Christ as his Lord and Savior in 1975. He was immediately confined in a mental asylum for his faith in Christ. Christopher responded quickly to the call of God and began to preach the Gospel. He was arrested several times and imprisoned for preaching the Gospel. After being threatened with execution, Christopher finally escaped to Sweden, where he was given political asylum. Today, Christopher resides in Pennsylvania with his wife, Britta. He has preached the Gospel in more than seventy nations, and more than 1400 churches have been started as fruit from his ministry, which is accompanied by signs, wonders, and miracles.

These individuals all turned adversities into opportunities. They took potential stumbling blocks and turned them into building blocks. They took what could have destroyed them, and with God's grace and help, turned it into something good.

As you explore the principles in this book, I pray that you will find peace in knowing that God is committed to you and your welfare, tenacity to cling to God in spite of great challenges, resilience to bounce back from the challenges of life, and courage to move forward with purpose and conviction. Finally, I pray that you will find assurance and strength in your life through the promise of Isaiah 54:17, which says, "'No weapon formed against you shall prosper, and every tongue which rises against you in judgment you shall condemn. This is the heritage of the servants of the Lord, and their righteousness is from Me,' says the Lord."

Chapter One

Can't I Just Have a Trouble-Free Life?

"Lower your expectations of earth. This isn't heaven, so don't expect it to be."

- Max Lucado

Key Thought: God never promised us a trouble-free life, but He did promise to help us through every adversity and challenge.

Preaching for the first time in a particular Southeast Asian country, I endeavored to make the simple point that all of us face problems in life and that God is committed to helping us through them. I intended to communicate, "Wouldn't it be wonderful if I could say a miracle prayer at the end of this service and have God bless each of you with a trouble-free life? And because of that great prayer, you would never face another problem as long as you live?" The hypothetical aspect of my statement must not have come across very clearly, because the people enthusiastically erupted in joy. I realized that what must have been conveyed through the interpreter was that I was *literally* going to pray for them, and that they would *actually* then experience a trouble-free, problem-free life. Talk about over-promising! It was certainly not my intention to mislead anyone or to set these folks up for great disappointment, so I began to clarify. Together, we looked at two powerful verses in the Bible that give us a realistic yet hopeful view of God and life.

> **Many are the afflictions of the righteous, but the LORD delivers him out of them all.**
>
> **Psalm 34:19**

> **These things I have spoken to you, that in Me you may have peace. In the world you will have tribulation; but be of good cheer, I have overcome the world.**
>
> **John 16:33**

Both of these passages clearly indicate one solid truth: if we live in this world, we are going to face some challenges. While we should be mindful that we will face problems in life, we don't have to be discouraged or fatalistic about it. Instead, we can choose to focus on the faithfulness and power of God that is also revealed in these verses. God has promised to deliver us from the afflictions of life, and Jesus has overcome the world!

Many people would prefer a problem-free life. I remember reading about a man who went down for prayer after a church service. The minister asked how he could pray for him. The man said, "I want you to pray that I'll never have any more trouble with the devil."

"Do you want me to pray that you'll die?" the minister responded.

The man responded, "No," so the minister informed him, "That's the only way in the world that you are never going to have any more trouble with the devil."[1]

---

[1] Kenneth E. Hagin, *Must Christians Suffer* (Tulsa, OK: Faith Library Publications, 1982), 10.

Similarly, Henry Ward Beecher once said, "You have come into a hard world. I know of only one easy place in it, and that is the grave." From this perspective, we can begin to get real with our faith. Faith is not wishful thinking. Faith is based on the truth of God's Word.

Perhaps there is something in all of us that desires to live in a utopia—to enjoy a perfect life free from inconvenience or anything that is uncomfortable or unpleasant. Who wouldn't like a perfect life, perfect marriage, perfect kids, perfect job, perfect church, and perfect friends? Perhaps hyper-idealism causes us to read the Bible selectively, filtering out the parts we don't want to hear and only focusing on those parts of Scripture that promise what we want. Perhaps this denial (ignoring scriptures we deem negative) is really based on fear and the erroneous belief that I can somehow control everything and every outcome in this world.

Have you ever thought, *If I can just do everything perfectly—make the right decision and do the right thing 100% of the time - then I'll never have a problem*? There's only been one person in all of human history who has done everything perfectly, who never sinned or made a mistake, who made the right decision, and did the right thing 100% of the time. His name is Jesus. And did *He* have a trouble-free life? Hardly.

- God sent His Son to earth, and the first thing an evil king did was put "a hit" out on Him. An assassination squad attempted to kill Jesus while He was still a small child.
- Mark's gospel gives this interesting perspective on how Jesus' own natural family perceived Him: "And when those who belonged to Him (His kinsmen) heard it, they went out to take Him by force, for they kept saying, He is out of His mind (beside Himself, deranged)!" (Mark 3:21, AMP).

- Jesus was reviled, hated, despised, and accused of being a blasphemer. On various occasions, people tried to kill Him.
- His close friends argued frequently. One of his associates eventually betrayed him and committed suicide.
- Eventually, Jesus was crucified.

Recognizing these facts will pretty much ruin anyone's plan to attain a problem-free life through personal perfection. If Jesus couldn't do it, neither can we.

In my younger years, I wasn't thrilled when I heard a respected spiritual leader say that the crises of life come to us all. Nor did I care for it when another minister wrote a book called *Ready or Not, Here Comes Trouble.*[2] But eventually I grew to learn that it's wishful thinking (based on hyper-idealism) that says, "I will never have a problem." On the other hand, faith—which is based on the reality of God's Word—says, "I may face problems, but my God is greater than any problem, and He will see me through."

The Bible teaches us to be realistically optimistic. If we are optimistic without being grounded in reality, we can easily become a Pollyanna type—naive, unrealistic, and with our head in the clouds. If we are realistic without being optimistic, we can easily end up jaded, cynical, pessimistic, and even fatalistic. Being realistically optimistic is consistent with Jesus' admonition to his disciples to "be as clever as snakes and as innocent as doves" (Matthew 10:16, NCV).

Let's look at this idea of realistic optimism as it pertains to marriage. Billy Graham once said, "For a married couple to expect perfection in each other is unrealistic." The Apostle Paul was even more blunt when he said, "...those who marry will face many troubles in this life..." (1 Corinthians

[2] Roy Hicks, *Ready or Not, Here Comes Trouble* (Tulsa, OK: Harrison House, 1980).

7:28, NIV). Does this mean that we should all expect to have an unbearably bad marriage, something akin to Armageddon? Not at all. We should aspire to have healthy, growing marriages. We should not, however, be shocked when we encounter issues that we have to work through, challenges that we have to overcome, and problems that we have to resolve. To go into marriage assuming it will be constant euphoria is to set ourselves up for disappointment.

It's vital for us to learn the balance between realism and optimism. In his book, Good to Great, Jim Collins recounts a conversation he had with Admiral Jim Stockdale, decorated war veteran and the highest-ranking U.S. military officer to be imprisoned during the Vietnam War. Stockdale was a prisoner of war for eight years and was tortured more than twenty times. As the commanding officer in that setting, Stockdale helped as many men survive as he could. Collins wrote, "What separates people, Stockdale taught me, is not the presence or absence of difficulty, but how they deal with the inevitable difficulties of life. In wrestling with life's challenges, the Stockdale Paradox (you must retain faith that you will prevail in the end and you must also confront the brutal facts of your current reality) has proved powerful for coming back from difficulties not weakened, but stronger...."[3]

As believers, we must do the same: confront the facts of our situation while still maintaining our faith in God. Others throughout history have also recognized the need to face reality and yet maintain faith.

President Theodore Roosevelt said it another way: "We must face the facts as they are. We must neither surrender ourselves to foolish optimism, nor succumb to a timid and ignoble pessimism." Roosevelt also said, "I wish to preach, not the doctrine of ignoble ease, but the doctrine of the

---

[3] Jim Collins, *Good to Great* (New York: HarperCollins Publishers, 2001), 85-86.

strenuous life; the life of toil and effort; of labor and strife; to preach that highest form of success which comes, not to the man who desires more easy peace, but to the man who does not shrink from danger, from hardship or from bitter toil, and who out of these wins the splendid ultimate triumph."

Winston Churchill modeled this realistic optimistic approach well. He was profoundly aware of the grave challenges faced by Great Britain in World War II, and yet he said, "I am an optimist. It does not seem too much use being anything else." Helen Keller stated, "A happy life consists not in the absence, but in the mastery of hardships." These men and women seemed to understand an important truth, one that we would all benefit from embracing.

God is not just the basis for our optimism, but He is also very much a part of our reality! God is real. His promises are real. His Presence is real. His power is real. Faith in God does not give us blanket immunity from all of the problems of the world, but it does give us an entirely different framework and perspective on how to deal with those problems. The faith component does not negate our doing our part, but it adds an element of reliance upon a God "who is able to do exceedingly abundantly above all that we ask or think, according to the power that works in us" (Ephesians 3:20).

So just how realistic is the Bible when it comes to facing adversity or the storms of life?

Proverbs 21:31 (NASB) says, "The horse is prepared for the day of battle, but victory belongs to the LORD." The Message Version renders that verse, "Do your best, prepare for the worst—then trust GOD to bring victory." Note that these people were admonished to prepare for battle. Faith in God is not an excuse to forgo proper preparation in the natural. Let me say that another way: faith does not mean we should be negligent in practical areas. Proverbs instructs us to remember that God is the One who ultimately brings victory, but we're also told to fortify ourselves in the natural.

Nehemiah had tremendous faith in God, but faith did not stop him from taking natural preparations and precautions while rebuilding the walls of Jerusalem. Consider the actions Nehemiah took based on his awareness of the threats against his people and the project.

> **From that day on, half of my men did the work while the other half held spears, shields, bows, and armor. The officers supported all the people of Judah, who were rebuilding the wall. The laborers who carried the loads worked with one hand and held a weapon with the other. Each of the builders had his sword strapped around his waist while he was building, and the trumpeter was beside me.**
>
> **Nehemiah 4:16-18 (HCSB)**

Nehemiah and his men believed that victory was from the Lord, but they still prepared themselves for the day of battle. While half of the men worked to build the wall, the other half stood guard with weapons. Similarly, when David faced Goliath he believed that God was with him, but he still selected five smooth stones to be used with his sling (see 1 Samuel 17:45-47). We are better served when we combine our faith in God with the natural resources and wisdom that God has given us. Using both the natural and the spiritual, we are better equipped to face life's problems.

Paul's Hindrance

Lest you think that problems were only in the lives of Old Testament believers, let's take a look at the Apostle Paul, who told believers to "be strong in the Lord and in the power of His might," and to "put on the whole armor of God..." (Ephesians 6:10-11). He also told Timothy to "be strong in the grace that is in Christ Jesus," and to "endure hardship as a good soldier of Jesus Christ" (2 Timothy 2:1, 3). Along with Barnabas, Paul went about "strengthening the souls of the disciples, exhorting them to continue in the faith, and saying, 'We must through many tribulations enter the kingdom of God'" (Acts 14:22).

Paul had a profound love for the churches he started. He would often go back to those congregations to provide further ministry and encouragement to them. After escaping Thessalonica in the midst of great danger, Paul longed to visit these fledgling believers again. In this case, Paul's desire was delayed. Things didn't always go the way Paul wanted them to go and circumstances were not always favorable for him. He referred to a hindrance that kept him from revisiting these believers on more than one occasion. He wrote, "Therefore we wanted to come to you—even I, Paul, time and again—but Satan hindered us" (1 Thessalonians 2:18).

The Greek word that Paul uses here that is translated "hindrance" means:

- to cut in on someone
- to impede one's course by cutting off his way
- to detain
- to thwart
- to impede someone by breaking up the road, or by placing an obstacle in their path

Have you ever felt detained? Impeded? Thwarted? That you had obstacles in your path?

Paul wasn't just hindered in getting to Thessalonica. He also acknowledged delays he faced in going to visit the believers in Rome:

- "I often planned to come to you (but was hindered until now), that I might have some fruit among you also, just as among the other Gentiles" (Romans 1:13).
- "...I also have been much hindered from coming to you" (Romans 15:22).

We know that Paul eventually made it back to Thessalonica, and he eventually made it to Rome. In both cases, however, it took him longer than he would have liked. It's important to understand that having faith does not mean that you never face trials; faith means that you persevere and continue to trust God in spite of the trials. It is important to not become weary or disillusioned when we face delays.

Paul attributed this particular hindrance to Satan, and most likely it had to do with persecution that Paul faced in various places for preaching the gospel. Sometimes Satan works through circumstances. The Bible tells us that Satan is "the god of this world" (2 Corinthians 4:4, NLT), and he does have influence in this realm. However, we should not exalt Satan or give him undue attention. He is not omniscient, omnipotent, or omnipresent, and he is a defeated enemy. Our focus should be predominantly on Jesus, and we should always focus on the fact that "He who is in you is greater than he who is in the world" (1 John 4:4).

We should not go through life preoccupied with the devil, but neither should we be "ignorant of his devices" (2 Corinthians 2:11). We should not be obsessed with or oblivious to our enemy. Either extreme puts us in a ditch. Not every problem we face in life is directly attributable to the devil; some things happen just because we live in a fallen and imperfect world that we share with other imperfect people. Regardless, though, of where problems come from, we have a God who has promised us that He will always be with us, and that He will help us, empower us, and deliver us.

Concluding Thought: God never promised us a trouble-free life, but He did promise to help us through every adversity and challenge.

Questions for Reflection and Discussion

1. The Bible says, "Many are the afflictions of the righteous, but the Lord delivers him out of them all" (Psalm 34:19). In spite of the Bible's clear teaching on this, do you ever find yourself shocked when you encounter a problem? In your opinion, do you or others seem to have some kind of subliminal belief that you should have a completely trouble-free life?
2. How realistic are you about life? Is your faith solidly based upon the Word of God, or do you sometimes find yourself operating in "wishful thinking" instead?
3. Jesus is the only perfect person who has ever lived, and yet He faced multiple adversities throughout His life. What are your reflections on that, and what lessons can you learn from that?
4. Go back and review the portion on the Stockdale Paradox, which is summed up as saying we must retain faith that we will prevail in the end, even as we confront the brutal facts of our current realities. Has that concept already been a part of your approach to life? If so, how has it worked for you? If not, do you feel that adopting that type of thinking would be helpful to you? Why or why not?

5. When you think about the hindrance that Paul faced in getting to Thessalonica and also the hindrances he encountered in his attempts to visit Rome, do any hindrances or delays that you have faced in life come to mind?
6. What has your perspective been on the nature of problems? Have you tended to see all problems as entirely demonic, all problems as entirely natural, or some blend thereof?

Chapter Two

Jonah's Storm

O Israel, thou hast destroyed thyself; but in me is thine help.
- Hosea 13:9 (KJV)

Key Thought: Jonah got into his storm because of disobedience. He got out of his storm through prayer, repentance, and consecration to do the will of God.

I'm not much of a handyman, but I vividly remember trying to tackle a particular project in the garage many years ago. I couldn't find the "chuck key" for the power drill (I needed to change the drill bit), so I decided to improvise. I took another drill bit, inserted the shank end into the tightening collar, held the other end—the one with the cutting edges—tightly in my hand, and pulled the trigger. If you know anything about power drills, you know that that is *not* the way to loosen the collar, but, rather, an invitation to pain and injury. The drill bit I was holding ripped through the skin on the palm of my hand. More than two decades later, I still have a scar there as a reminder of my foolishness.

I didn't hurt myself on purpose. But even when a bad decision is completely unintentional—an accident—there can still be consequences. The word "accident" is defined as "an unforeseen and unplanned event or circumstance" and an "unfortunate event resulting especially from carelessness or ignorance."[4] Accidents often have the same dire consequences as intentional bad decisions, but accidents are typically unforeseen and unplanned.

Should I have looked for a deep spiritual reason for my accident with the drill bit? Did God sovereignly orchestrate my bad decision to teach me a lesson? Did the devil diabolically scheme to work his sinister plan against me? The answer to all of these questions is, no. Proverbs 19:3 (MSG) says, "People ruin their lives by their own stupidity, so why does God always get blamed?" God also said, "My people are destroyed for lack of knowledge" (Hosea 4:6). I simply made a really bad decision. I acted unwisely, used that power drill contrary to its design, and suffered an unfortunate consequence.

I doubt anyone would accuse me of being "disobedient" in that situation. Disobedience usually has the connotation of something that is more willful, more intentionally defiant. I certainly had no malicious intention in acting contrary to the operating instructions for that drill, but regardless of how naive and innocent my ignorance may have been, I suffered the same consequences as if it had been deliberate rebellion on my part. The physical injury was relatively minor, but I felt embarrassed about my ignorance and carelessness. I was tempted to be down on myself, but I had to shake it off and remember, in the future, to respect power tools and use them properly.

We might hate to admit it—it can be hard on our pride—but sometimes we create problems for ourselves. We can be our own worst enemy, and sometimes we sabotage our own success. I remember a husband who

---

[4] *Merriam-Webster.com,* s.v. "accident." http://www.merriam-webster.com/dictionary/accident

thought his wife was the problem, when really he had created his own problems. The husband had abused his wife and was bemoaning his wife's decision to leave him. He arrogantly challenged me to tell her, based on his understanding of the Bible, that she was to return and submit to him. I told him that the Bible was already operative in this situation: "He who troubles his own house will inherit the wind" (Proverbs 11:29). That wasn't what he wanted to hear, but it is what he—because of his blind arrogance—needed to hear.

Another man once told me, "The devil is really attacking my marriage." Having counseled him and his wife, I knew that he had been consistently unkind, neglectful, and inconsiderate toward his wife. I was tempted to tell him, "Perhaps you're making it easy for the devil to attack your marriage because you're giving him all the ammunition he needs." I recognize that there can be valid spiritual attacks, but I also recognize that sometimes blaming the devil can be an easy cop-out from taking responsibility for our contribution to the problem.

The simple point is this: actions have consequences. Galatians 6:8 says, "He who sows to his flesh will of the flesh reap corruption." If we've created our own storm, we need to face the truth and take ownership of our actions. This doesn't mean we have to wallow in perpetual condemnation; certainly we should receive God's forgiveness, seek the forgiveness of others when appropriate, and forgive ourselves. Facing the truth, though, means that we don't seek to blame God or the devil; instead, we are honest with others and ourselves.

Someone once told me, "God put me through a divorce to teach me some things." I have a problem with making God the author of divorce. Of course, God always wants to teach us things, and we can certainly learn from all kinds of circumstances. But we don't need to make God the scapegoat in these types of situations. God is the author of our solutions, not our problems!

Some bad decisions are unintentional. Other times, people knowingly make bad decisions. We call that *disobedience*, a term that implies a willful neglect of doing what one knows is right, a refusal to do what one knows he should, or a conscious choice to do something one knows is wrong. People who choose to make bad decisions don't usually think they are "choosing" the consequences that will follow, but they are choosing a course of action that ends up producing those consequences. Even so, they often act surprised when those inevitable consequences occur. Some people become truly sorry that they disobeyed; others are just sorry they got caught or are sorry that they have to experience the negative fallout from their choices.

Lessons from Jonah's Storm

The Bible is full of examples of people who made choices and faced the consequences of their choices. If you grew up attending Sunday school or church, you've no doubt heard of Jonah. He was a prophet of God in ancient Israel. God gave him a very clear assignment: "Arise, go to Nineveh, that great city, and cry against it; for their wickedness is come up before Me" (Jonah 1:2). God spoke plainly to Jonah, and Jonah knew exactly what God wanted him to do. But instead of obeying God, Jonah decided to do something quite different.

> **But Jonah rose up to flee unto Tarshish from the presence of the LORD, and went *down* to Joppa; and he found a ship going to Tarshish: so he paid the fare thereof, and went *down* into it, to go with them unto Tarshish from the presence of the LORD.**
> **But the LORD sent out a great wind into the sea, and there was a mighty tempest in the sea, so that the ship was like to be broken.**

Then the mariners were afraid, and cried every man unto his god, and cast forth the wares that were in the ship into the sea, to lighten it of them. But Jonah was gone *down* into the sides of the ship; and he lay, and was fast asleep.

Jonah 1:3-5 (KJV emphasis mine)

Just how much was Jonah trying to get away from God's will? Ninevah, where Jonah was supposed to go, was located in modern-day Iraq. Tarshish, where Jonah was heading, is believed to have been in modern-day Spain. In other words, Jonah was heading in the exact opposite direction of where God had told him to go.

I encourage you to read the entire book of Jonah, but first notice the word "down" in verses 3-5. Keep this in mind: whenever you are running away from God, you are in the process of going down, down, down. Jonah was running away from God, and he actually told others on the boat that he was doing so. Jonah 1:10 says, "For the men knew that he fled from the presence of the LORD, because he had told them."

So there's Jonah, running from God, telling people he's running from God, and a great storm overtakes the boat. The next thing we know, Jonah (believed by those on board to be the reason for the storm) has been thrown off the ship and swallowed by a great fish.

Now the LORD had prepared a great fish to swallow Jonah. And Jonah was in the belly of the fish three days and three nights. Then Jonah prayed to the LORD his God from the fish's belly.

Jonah 1:17-2:1 (KJV)

I'm sure being inside of a fish wasn't very funny to Jonah, but I find the way Jonah responded a bit humorous because of how typical his reaction is. Jonah had been using all of his efforts to get away from God's plan for his life, but as soon as he got in really big trouble…he prayed. Too many

Christians are quite content to do their own thing and go their own way, but when trouble hits, *then* they pray!

What exactly did Jonah pray? The prophet was very honest about the seriousness of his circumstances—he was not in a state of denial. Jonah graphically described his problem, but more importantly he consecrated himself to God, trusted in God's mercy, and committed himself to following the will of God for his life.

I cried out to the LORD in my great trouble,
and he answered me.
I called to you from the land of the dead,
and LORD, you heard me!
You threw me into the ocean depths,
and I sank down to the heart of the sea.
The mighty waters engulfed me;
I was buried beneath your wild and stormy waves.
Then I said, "O LORD, you have driven me from your presence.
Yet I will look once more toward your holy Temple."
I sank beneath the waves,
and the waters closed over me.
Seaweed wrapped itself around my head.
I sank down to the very roots of the mountains.
I was imprisoned in the earth,
whose gates lock shut forever.
But you, O LORD my God,
snatched me from the jaws of death!
As my life was slipping away,
I remembered the LORD.
And my earnest prayer went out to you
in your holy Temple.

Those who worship false gods
turn their backs on all God's mercies.
But I will offer sacrifices to you with songs of praise,
and I will fulfill all my vows.
For my salvation comes from the LORD alone.

Jonah 2:2-9 (NLT)

Jonah cried out in his distress, and the Lord heard him. Jonah got out of the storm, got out of the fish, and here's what happened next.

Now the word of the LORD came to Jonah the second time, saying, "Arise, go to Nineveh, that great city, and preach to it the message that I tell you." So Jonah arose and went to Nineveh, according to the word of the LORD.

Jonah 3:1-3

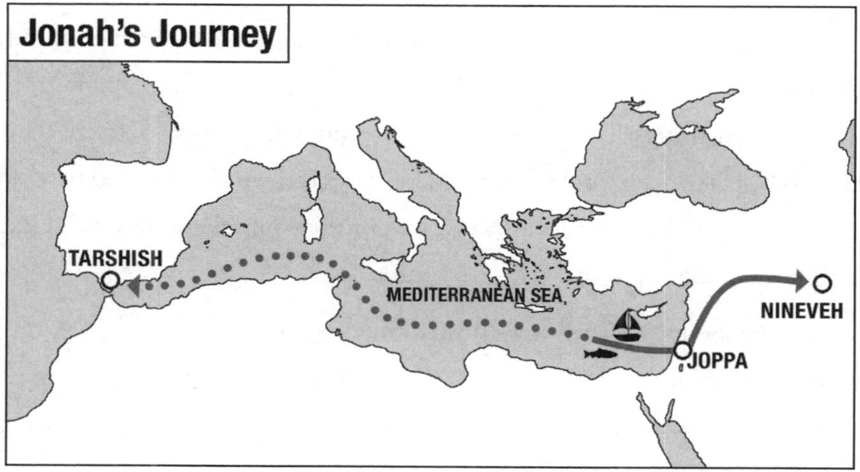

Jonah got a second chance! He suffered consequences because of his initial disobedience, but God gave him a second chance. Thank God for His mercy that endures forever. Jonah made it to the place God had originally intended and preached to the people as he had been instructed, and the people repented and were spared!

Prayer Isn't Just for Emergencies

Jonah isn't the only one to have prayed his way out of self-inflicted trouble. Another "...then he prayed" passage is found in the book of Psalms.

Fools, because of their transgression,
And because of their iniquities, were afflicted.
Then they cried out to the LORD in their trouble,
And He saved them out of their distresses.
He sent His word and healed them,
And delivered them from their destructions.

Psalm 107:17, 19-20

As much as I appreciate the fresh opportunity that Jonah received, I've learned that prayer isn't intended to be a last resort—a "panic button" we hit when things have gone wrong. It's better to pray proactively than reactively. How many problems could be averted if we sought God first? If we prayed first? If we obeyed first? If we got the counsel and mind of God before we made decisions?

It's far better to have loving fellowship with God on a regular, ongoing basis than to speak to Him only in emergencies or when we need something. However, there's absolutely nothing wrong with praying when there is a problem—I can't think of a better thing to do.

Don't hesitate to call on God even if you neglected your relationship with Him prior to a problem arising. He still loves you and He wants to help you, not condemn you. Don't allow guilt and condemnation to keep you away from God. Don't run away from Him when you need Him the most.

It does no good to beat yourself up over "what might have been" or "what could/should have been." Like Jonah, we must deal with reality as it is, and look to God for His mercy and help to get us through the storm. Hebrews 4:16 (NLT) says, "Let us come boldly to the throne of our gracious God. There we will receive his mercy, and we will find grace to help us when we need it most." If you've gotten into a storm because of some type of disobedience in your life, don't just be sorry that you've experienced negative consequences, but let your heart be truly tender toward God. Don't just be sorry that you've been caught, but yield your heart completely to God and become eagerly willing to do His will.

You Can't Change the Past

Even if we've missed it in the past, we don't have to wallow in regret over past failures. That is not God's will for you! If there's something that can be recovered and restored from past mistakes (and often there is), that's great. Go for it. My wife, Lisa, says, "What God doesn't ordain, He redeems." In other words, when something happens that is not the will of God, it doesn't mean that life is over for us. God will work—if we allow Him—even in terrible situations, to bring out the maximum benefit.

Instead of looking back at your life with immobilizing sorrow, receive God's mercy and go forward. But go forward wiser than before and with a commitment to honor God and to do things His way from now on. Proverbs 13:15 says, "Good understanding giveth favour: but the way of transgressors is hard" (KJV). If you have experienced some hardness in your life because of transgressions you've made, learn from that and say with David, "Before I was afflicted I went astray, But now I keep Your word" (Psalm 119:67).

Consider Solomon's admonition:

> **How long, you simple ones, will you love simplicity? For scorners delight in their scorning, and fools hate knowledge.**
> **Turn at my rebuke; surely I will pour out my spirit on you; I will make my words known to you.**
> **Because I have called and you refused, I have stretched out my hand and no one regarded, because you disdained all my counsel, and would have none of my rebuke, I also will laugh at your calamity; I will mock when your terror comes, when your terror comes like a storm, and your destruction comes like a whirlwind, when distress and anguish come upon you.**
> **Then they will call on me, but I will not answer; they will seek me diligently, but they will not find me.**
> **Because they hated knowledge and did not choose the fear of the LORD,**
> **they would have none of my counsel and despised my every rebuke.**
> **Therefore they shall eat the fruit of their own way, and be filled to the full with their own fancies.**
> **For the turning away of the simple will slay them, and the complacency of fools will destroy them; but whoever listens to me will dwell safely, and will be secure, without fear of evil.**
>
> **Proverbs 1:22-33**

Regardless of your past, you have an opportunity right now to get a brand new start in life. God's mercies are new every morning (Lamentations

3:22-23). Make the decision right now to embrace Wisdom's counsel and to begin living a life of uncompromising obedience to God and His Word. What does God promise when you do that? He says that you will dwell safely, be secure, and live without fear of evil.

Concluding Thought: Jonah got into his storm because of disobedience. He got out of his storm through prayer, repentance, and consecration to do the will of God.

Questions for Reflection and Discussion

1. Have you ever felt like Jonah? Has there ever been something that you knew God wanted you to do—or something that was the right thing to do—but you simply did not want to do it?
2. What was your "Jonah experience" like and when did you turn your heart back to God?
3. Have you ever blamed God or the devil for a situation that was really of your own making? What made you face up to the truth?
4. Have you ever had trouble forgiving yourself for a past mistake? How did you come to the place where you could truly receive God's forgiveness and release yourself from the condemnation and shame of the past?
5. Have you ever had to go to others who had been adversely affected by a bad decision or actions on your part and ask their forgiveness? What happened as a result?

6. Have you ever gotten a "do over" like Jonah did? Have you ever had an opportunity to do something right after you'd failed the first time? How did that work for you and what were the results? What did you do differently the second time?

Chapter Three

The Storm of the Disciples

When the storms of life come, the wicked are whirled away, but the godly have a lasting foundation.

Proverbs 10:25, NLT

Key Thought: The disciples got into their storm when they were doing exactly what Jesus told them to do. They got out of their storm when spiritual authority was exercised and the Word of God was powerfully declared.

In the previous chapter, we discussed problems that result from disobedience or bad decisions on our part. We learned that while we need to face the truth and take responsibility for our own actions when we've missed it, we also need to forgive ourselves and move forward into God's good plan for our lives. In this chapter, we will discover that not every problem we encounter is due to a mistake we've made—not every storm is "a Jonah storm."

There has been a tendency among some Christians to assume that people who are facing a hindrance or negative circumstance must lack faith, have sin in their life, or be out of the will of God. Let's make this even more personal. If you are facing hindrances, challenges, or obstacles in your life, do you automatically assume that you lack faith, have sin in your life, or are out of the will of God?

When facing problems, do we tell ourselves that God does not love us as much as those who aren't facing the problems we are? Do we falsely believe that we are somehow a second-class Christian or an inferior believer? We must be diligent to guard ourselves against degrading, self-condemning thinking. Problems, or storms, come for many reasons, and we must be careful not to have a one-dimensional perspective.

It is true that storms can come as a result of disobedience in our lives. It is equally true that storms can come when we've done nothing wrong. In fact, storms can come when we've done something *right*!

Jonah is an example of one type of storm, but let's look at a totally different storm—one that involved Jesus' own disciples. In Mark 4, Jesus was teaching by the Sea of Galilee. On this particular day, he had shared the parable of the sower. What followed is truly amazing!

> **On the same day, when evening had come, He [Jesus] said to them, "Let us cross over to the other side." Now when they had left the multitude, they took Him along in the boat as He was. And other little boats were also with Him. And a great windstorm arose, and the waves beat into the boat, so that it was already filling. But He was in the stern, asleep on a pillow. And they awoke Him and said to Him, "Teacher, do You not care that we are perishing?"**
>
> **Then He arose and rebuked the wind, and said to the sea, "Peace, be still!" And the wind ceased and there was a great calm. But He said to them, "Why are you so fearful? How is it that you have**

no faith?" And they feared exceedingly, and said to one another, "Who can this be, that even the wind and the sea obey Him!"

Mark 4:35-41

We've already seen how Jonah got into trouble because he was out of the will of God. Now we're seeing how the disciples encountered adversity when they were doing exactly what Jesus told them to do. Simply put, this shows us that there are two times in our lives when we can face difficulties—when we're *out* of the will of God, and when we're *in* the will of God. Or, to say it another way, *at any given time!*

This truth might bother the person who wants a guarantee of a trouble-free life, but our real comfort is in knowing that God is greater than any difficulty we will ever face. He is completely committed to us, and He will lead us by His grace through every challenge of life. As Isaiah 43:2 (NLT) says, "When you go through deep waters, I will be with you. When you go through rivers of difficulty, you will not drown. When you walk through the fire of oppression, you will not be burned up; the flames will not consume you."

Let's examine what happened in Mark chapter 4.

1. Jesus gave a directive, "Let's cross over to the other side."
2. The disciples did precisely what Jesus told them to do. If you do what Jesus says, you are 100% in the will of God.
3. A great storm arose. This wasn't a minor storm; this one was filling the boat with water, and even professional fishermen—men who knew those waters and had been in storms before—were terrified.
4. Jesus was asleep in a small boat that was being battered and was filling with water. He must have really known how to rest in

God! Psalm 127:2 says, "He gives His beloved sleep." Proverbs 3:24 tells us, "When you lie down, you will not be afraid; Yes, you will lie down and your sleep will be sweet."

5. The disciples were terrified. They asked, "Teacher, do You not care that we are perishing?" When we are facing a crisis, there are two things we need to avoid:

- Avoid assuming that God does not care. Don't ever interpret God's love for you in the light of the circumstance you are facing. For example, don't say, "If God really loved me, I wouldn't be facing this problem. Therefore, He must not love me."
- Avoid assuming that you're going to experience a worst-case scenario as an outcome. This is called catastrophic thinking. Why not assume that God will influence the outcome in a positive way?

6. Jesus spoke to the storm. He exercised spiritual authority through His spoken word. Jesus told His disciples that their words could carry spiritual authority as well. In Mark 11:23 he said, "For assuredly, I say to you, whoever says to this mountain, 'Be removed and be cast into the sea,' and does not doubt in his heart, but believes that those things he says will be done, he will have whatever he says."
7. The disciples were awestruck by the power released through Jesus' spoken word. Jesus and his disciples made it safely to the other side of the Sea of Galilee, and Jesus ministered deliverance to a man possessed by an evil spirit (Mark 5:1-19).

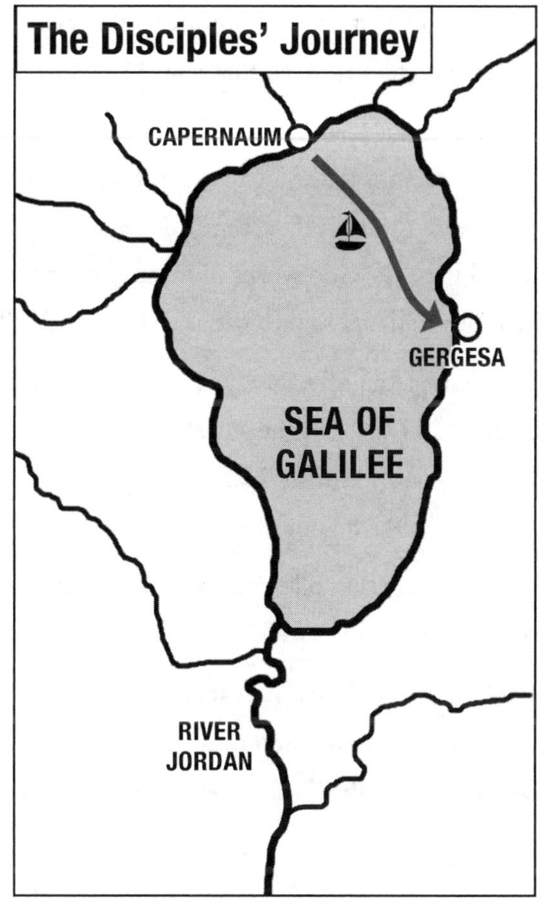

What Jesus Did Not Do

We've seen what Jesus did when He encountered this storm, but it's also important to see what Jesus did *not* do.

First, Jesus did not assume that one of His disciples had sinned, thus "opening the door" to this storm. He did not line the disciples up and say, "Alright, one of you guys has obviously sinned or we would not be in the middle of this storm. Go ahead and confess. Whose fault is this? Which one of you is responsible for this storm?" Jesus understood the reality of life—that bad things can happen even when you're trying to do a good thing. Encountering adversity doesn't automatically mean you've done bad things, and it certainly doesn't mean that you're a bad person.

Second, Jesus did not assume that this storm was some kind of gift from God to teach them a lesson or to teach them patience. He did not believe that they were to passively accept this storm and simply see what happened. He did not say, "God works in mysterious ways." No, Jesus got up and rebuked the wind and said to the sea, "Peace, be still!"

Jesus did not adopt the oft-embraced view that whatever happens in life is from God. If God *had* sent the storm, then Jesus rebuked the will of God when He rebuked the storm. No! Jesus clearly understood that not many circumstances in life are not from God.

Consider how clearly the following verses illustrate the stark contrast between the benevolent work of God and the destructive work of Satan.

> **...how God anointed Jesus of Nazareth with the Holy Spirit and with power, who went about doing good and healing all who were oppressed by the devil, for God was with Him.**
>
> **Acts 10:38**

> **For this purpose the Son of God was manifested, that He might destroy the works of the devil.**
>
> **1 John 3:8**

> **Therefore submit to God. Resist the devil and he will flee from you.**
>
> **James 4:7**

If God is doing something in our lives, we want to receive it, accept it, and submit to it. However, if an activity is not of God, we are to resist it and stand against it with every fiber of our being. How do we tell the difference? One great guideline is what Jesus said in John 10:10: "The thief does not come except to steal, and to kill, and to destroy. I have come that they may have life, and that they may have it more abundantly."

I'm not implying that every single negative thing in life is "a work of the devil." That flat tire your car had was most likely the result of running over a nail, not a demonic attack. We don't need to get spooky and over-spiritualize every situation, and let's not give Satan more credit than he deserves. The Bible doesn't explicitly say whether this storm was entirely natural or if there was a spiritual aspect behind it, but we do know that this storm stood between Jesus and the man with an unclean spirit, who responded to Jesus by saying, "My name is Legion; for we are many" (Mark 5:9). Because the storm stood between Jesus and ministering deliverance to a needy man, Jesus rebuked the storm and passed to the other side of the sea.

We can be assured that those demonic forces did not want Jesus arriving on that shore to set that man free, and we also know that Satan and his forces want to fight any advancement of the Word of God because they fear it so greatly. Satan knows that when individuals embrace the truth of God's Word, they get free and his grip over their lives is broken.

I am amazed at how often people attribute natural disasters and destructive events to God. If they don't overtly blame God, they play theological word games and proclaim that "God is in control." That's true, of course, in a general way, but such a statement can certainly leave a wrong impression. God is in control, ultimately, in an over-arching sense, but that doesn't mean that God is ordaining and causing natural disasters or violent tragedies here on earth.

If everything that happened here on earth was being "controlled" by God—as though He was some kind of great, micro-managing puppeteer—then Jesus would not have instructed us to pray: "Your kingdom come. Your will be done on earth as it is in heaven" (Matthew 6:10). Obviously, the will of God is often not done here on earth.

Attributing every earthly occurrence to God is not supported by Scripture or by common sense. Jesus did not consider the storm in Mark chapter 4 to have been sent by God, and He actively (under the anointing of the Holy Spirit) worked against sickness, oppression, and bondage.

Even people who embrace an extreme view of sovereignty (a view that completely disregards man's free will) wouldn't passively submit to things they felt they could change. For example, if a fire started in their house and they had a hose, they wouldn't say, "Well, this fire must be from God, so we'll just see what happens." No, they'd begin spraying the fire with water! If they were diagnosed with a disease, they would see if something could be done about it. If they had a tumor and their doctor said it could be removed, they wouldn't say, "I don't know... maybe God wants me to have this tumor."

Extreme passivity is not consistent with Scripture or reason. Jesus was certainly not passive when it came to the storm He encountered. I understand that we can't control every situation on planet earth, but there are definitely some things that our faith, our decisions, and our actions can affect. Reinhold Niebuhr expressed the importance of knowing the difference between what we can change and what we can't in what is now commonly called "The Serenity Prayer." The modern version of this prayer states, "God grant me the serenity to accept the things I cannot change; courage to change the things I can; and wisdom to know the difference."

I don't want to assume that I'm a helpless victim or adopt an attitude of passivity when God has given us powerful spiritual weapons. God has given us the Name of Jesus, the Word of God, the Armor of God, the gifts of the Holy Spirit, and the power of prayer. When I'm obeying God and seeking to do His will and a storm comes to hinder me, I want to use every tool I have at my disposal—both natural and spiritual—to overcome that obstacle and press on into the fullness of God's plan for my life.

What Jesus Explained Right Before the Storm

On the very day the disciples encountered the storm, Jesus had shared some very important spiritual truths in what we call "The Parable of the Sower." I encourage you to read everything Jesus taught leading up to His encounter with the storm (Mark 4:1-34), but let me highlight part of it.

> **The sower sows the word. And these are the ones by the wayside where the word is sown. When they hear, Satan comes immediately and takes away the word that was sown in their hearts. These likewise are the ones sown on stony ground who, when they hear the word, immediately receive it with gladness; and they have no root in themselves, and so endure only for a time. Afterward, when tribulation or persecution arises for the word's sake, immediately they stumble.**
>
> **Mark 4:14-17**

Jesus had spoken the word, "Let us cross over to the other side." When the disciples acted accordingly, opposition was encountered. The storm was a hindrance to Jesus' directive that would lead Him to the demoniac. Satan knew that wherever Jesus went, people were set free. He did not want to lose control of that possessed man on the other side of the Sea of Galilee that he had afflicted for so long. Tribulation arose for the Word's sake, and immediately the disciples stumbled through fear. Jesus, however, stood up and reinforced the word He had spoken with the command, "Peace, be still."

Sometimes believers are tested in the area that they have just received insight or teaching on, because Satan comes immediately to steal the

Word. Other times, it seems that circumstances are tailor-made to hinder you in the very thing you are striving to achieve. A student in Bible school once noted that when he was taught certain subjects, challenges directly related to the word he was receiving would come into his life. He observed that when he took the class "Christ the Healer," he was attacked with sickness, and when he took the class "God's Laws of Prosperity," he went broke. He then jokingly added that when he studied fasting in the Bible that he actually gained weight (he realized that was because of his diet, not because of any spiritual attack).

The enemy will attempt to bring thoughts and/or circumstances into your life to dishearten you and get you to relinquish your hold on the Word of God. Many people who have accepted Jesus as Savior are shortly thereafter bombarded with the thought, "You didn't really get saved...if you had gotten saved, you wouldn't have had that bad thought." Or, "If you were really a Christian, you wouldn't have done that wrong thing."

Remember that Satan's goal is to take away the Word that has been sown into your heart and to discourage you through tribulations or persecutions that arise for the Word's sake. Why is he so intent upon that? Consider the following that reveals how God has invested His power in His word:

- Hebrews 11:3 says, "By faith we understand that the worlds were framed by the word of God...."
- His words "are life to those who find them, and health to all their flesh" (Proverbs 4:22).
- Jeremiah 1:12 (AMP) says, "I am alert and active, watching over My word to perform it."
- "No word from God shall be without power or impossible of fulfillment" (Luke 1:37, AMP).

- "Faith comes by hearing, and hearing by the word of God" (Romans 10:17).
- 1 Thessalonians 2:13 (AMP) says, "…the Word of God...is effectually at work in you who believe [exercising its superhuman power in those who adhere to and trust in and rely on it]."

With God's very own power residing in His Word, it's no wonder our adversary works so hard to keep us from receiving God's Word and making it the basis for our thoughts and actions. Don't flatter yourself by thinking that Satan is overly impressed with or concerned about you personally; it's the Word he's after. He's not bothered by *you*, per se, but he hates when believers gets established in and act upon the Word of the Living God. That Word is "the sword of the Spirit" (Ephesians 6:17), and Satan knows that if you get full of the Word, transformed by the Word, and empowered by the Word, you are going to be unstoppable.

Let's look at a hypothetical example of this principle in action. Let's say that Frank has never tithed or generously supported the Lord's work. Frank hears his pastor teach on giving, and God convicts his heart about getting involved with Heaven's stewardship plan. The Word he has received inspires his faith, but Frank's flesh and mind are giving him fits about it. Can you imagine the battle going on above his shoulders? *You can't give 10% of your income to the church. That's crazy. You'll go broke. You'll lose everything you have.* (Let me assure you that Satan does not want to see believers tithing or giving generously. He'd like to see all Christians be very stingy and see churches and ministries financially strapped.)

Frank decides, though, to take God at His Word and begins to tithe. He's glad he's acting on the Word, and expects God to bless him. Shortly thereafter, the water pump goes out on his car and sets him back $275. That may be an entirely natural occurrence, but don't think that the enemy is going to let this opportunity go to waste! Frank begins to face thoughts, *How's that tithing thing working for you? You should have kept that money you gave to the church. Obviously, you wasted your money, and now you're moving backward financially. You'd better quit tithing before you really get in trouble.*

Satan has come for the Word's sake. The water pump didn't go out because Frank was in disobedience; it probably went out because it was worn out. But the spiritual attack that now comes to Frank's mind is based on his commitment and determination to obey God. Frank can yield to the negative thoughts and the pressure he's feeling and let go of God's Word. Or he can rise up in faith and commit to obeying God's Word. Holding on to God's Word, and persevering and continuing in faith is what causes us to walk in victory!

Imagine Frank taking this approach in prayer: "Heavenly Father, I recently committed to tithe and be the generous person You've called me to be. This setback will not throw me off track. I will not succumb to thoughts of doubt, fear, or failure. I take my stand upon Your Word, and I know that You are faithful to bless and prosper me. I have received Your Word on tithing and giving, and I will persevere in obedience to You. Thank You that the windows of Heaven are open to me and that You are pouring out blessings in my life that I won't have room enough to contain. I rebuke lack and poverty, and I thank You that You give me wisdom to manage my resources wisely for Your glory, and that You grant favor, enabling me to prosper in every area of my life. In Jesus' Name I pray. Amen."

If Frank will continue to stand strong in faith, he will establish a consistent lifestyle of wise stewardship and generosity based on the Word of God. Challenges, no doubt, will come from time to time, but God will bless him and make him a blessing. This same principle applies to all believers in every area of life. We must not assume that the challenges we face are of our own making or are a result of wrongdoing. If we are following God's Word and using wisdom, we must continue to stand firm when the storms begin to rage. Using the natural and spiritual resources God has given us, we, too, will arrive safely on the other side.

Concluding Thought: The disciples got into their storm when they were doing exactly what Jesus told them to do. They got out of their storm when spiritual authority was exercised and the Word of God was powerfully declared.

Questions for Reflection and Discussion

1, Have you ever believed or felt that when you had a problem, it was automatically due to some mistake, sin, or lack of faith in your own life? What effect did that misbelief have on you?

2. Have you ever found yourself falling prey to the trap of interpreting God's love for you in the light of your circumstances? In other words, have you ever felt that encountering problems somehow indicated that God didn't love you or wasn't being faithful to you? If so, how did you deal with those thoughts?

3. When you think of Jesus speaking to the storm and consider Mark 11:23 ("Whoever says to this mountain, 'Be removed and be cast into the sea,' and does not doubt in his heart, but believes that those things he says will be done, he will have whatever he says"), does it cause you to think of any of life's circumstances or situations that you should be speaking to in faith?

4. Apparently Jesus did not believe that every circumstance in life is from God and to be passively received. He actively resisted and worked against certain things. How does this principle apply to you? What do you receive and what do you resist? Scripturally, how are we to tell the difference?
5. How would you respond to someone who says that natural disasters or violent acts upon the earth are the will of God? How does this particular belief impact the way people perceive God, and what Scriptures might you share to refute such an idea?
6. Why would the enemy fight so hard to keep believers from embracing the Word of God in faith and making it the basis for their thoughts and actions?

Chapter Four

Paul's Storm

"Endurance is not just the ability to bear a hard thing, but to turn it into glory."

- William Barclay

Key Thought: Paul got into his storm because of the disobedience of others. He got out of his storm through his persevering, enduring faith in God.

We've looked at one storm that came because of personal *disobedience* (Jonah), and another storm that came in the midst of perfect personal *obedience* (the disciples). There is a third great storm in the Bible from which we can derive another important lesson: adversity can also come into our lives when *other people are disobedient*. Have you ever been negatively affected because of the wrong choices and wrong actions of others?

Consider the story of a great storm encountered by the Apostle Paul in Acts chapter 27. Earlier, in Acts 21, Paul had been arrested in Jerusalem. When formal charges were finally brought against Paul, the accusers claimed, "We have found this man a plague, a creator of dissension among all the Jews throughout the world, and a ringleader of the sect of the Nazarenes" (Acts 24:5). Paul realized that he would not receive a fair trial due to their religious prejudices, so he exercised his right as a Roman citizen and appealed his case to Caesar (Acts 25:12). Having made that petition, it became the responsibility of the Roman authorities to transport Paul to Rome to stand trial. This led to an excruciating experience in Paul's life, and the entire 27th chapter of Acts is devoted to the horrific, lengthy storm that he encountered.

The westward journey by sea toward Rome was difficult, and the ship on which Paul was sailing stopped briefly along the way at a port named Fair Havens on the Island of Crete. From here, a decision had to be made. Would they stay put for the winter, or sail on to find a better harbor? Both options presented risks. Let's read what happened.

> **Now when much time had been spent, and sailing was now dangerous because the Fast was already over, Paul advised them, saying, "Men, I perceive that this voyage will end with disaster and much loss, not only of the cargo and ship, but also our lives." Nevertheless the centurion was more persuaded by the helmsman and the owner of the ship than by the things spoken by Paul. And because the harbor was not suitable to winter in, the majority advised to set sail from there also, if by any means they could reach Phoenix, a harbor of Crete opening toward the southwest and northwest, and winter there.**
>
> **When the south wind blew softly, supposing that they had obtained their desire, putting out to sea, they sailed close by Crete. But not long after, a tempestuous head wind arose, called Euroclydon.**
>
> **Acts 27:9-14**

From there, they were violently driven by the storm out into the sea, but let's review what has happened so far.

1. Paul "perceived" something. He warned his fellow travelers that there would be great danger ahead if they sailed. Paul was neither a mariner nor a meteorologist, but he knew the Holy Spirit. Led by the Spirit, Paul issued his warning.
2. As a prisoner, Paul did not have the authority to make the decision. Others expressed their wishes, and the majority prevailed. This is a good reminder that the majority is not always right. It also reminds us that we can't control or override the free will of other people.
3. When they set sail, they initially encountered favorable circumstances. They mistakenly interpreted this to mean that they had made the right decision. However, initial favorable results do not confirm that a good decision has been made. In this case, smooth sailing turned into a terrible storm very quickly.
4. Finally, Paul's prediction began to come to pass. The NLT renders verse 14, "The weather changed abruptly, and a wind of typhoon strength (called a "northeaster") burst across the island and blew us out to sea."

The storm that Paul and the others encountered went on for two weeks! Can you imagine being on a storm-tossed ship for that long? Lisa and I, along with others in our tour group, recently took an eighty-seven foot boat from the coast of Turkey (near ancient Ephesus) out to the Island of Patmos. This is north of where Paul would have been sailing—and we had some very rough water. Even though our boat ride was a mere four hours, moe than half of our passengers became sick in a very short time. It was a miserable experience for many of us on board, and Paul's ordeal—276 were on his ship—would have been multiplied times worse.

Now when neither sun nor stars appeared for many days, and no small tempest beat on us, all hope that we would be saved was finally given up.

> **But after long abstinence from food, then Paul stood in the midst of them and said, "Men, you should have listened to me, and not have sailed from Crete and incurred this disaster and loss. And now I urge you to take heart, for there will be no loss of life among you, but only of the ship. For there stood by me this night an angel of the God to whom I belong and whom I serve, saying, 'Do not be afraid, Paul; you must be brought before Caesar; and indeed God has granted you all those who sail with you.' Therefore take heart, men, for I believe God that it will be just as it was told me."**
>
> **Acts 27:20-25**

Isn't that something? Having heard from the angel, Paul essentially told the others on board, "I told you so!" Even though God promised deliverance with no fatalities, it was not going to be a fairy tale ending. The journey ended violently, with the ship breaking apart and everyone having to swim ashore. Still, that beats the ship sinking at sea with everyone drowning, doesn't it?

A Hard Landing

Have you ever made it through a situation and were thankful for making it through, but the way the situation ended was still not easy? That's exactly what Paul and the others experienced at the end of the storm.

When morning dawned, they didn't recognize the coastline, but they saw a bay with a beach and wondered if they could get to shore by running the ship aground. So they cut off the anchors and left them in the sea. Then they lowered the rudders, raised the foresail, and headed toward shore. But they hit a shoal and ran the ship aground too soon. The bow of the ship stuck fast, while the stern was repeatedly smashed by the force of the waves and began to break apart.

The soldiers wanted to kill the prisoners to make sure they didn't swim ashore and escape. But the commanding officer wanted to spare Paul, so he didn't let them carry out their plan. Then he ordered all who could swim to jump overboard first and make for land. The others held onto planks or debris from the broken ship. So everyone escaped safely to shore.

Acts 27:39-44 (NLT)

Not only was Paul subjected to two weeks of a terrible storm at sea, the destruction of the ship, and a swim to shore, but when he got to shore, he was exposed to the elements (rain and cold) and was bitten by a viper as he laid wood on the fire. It's a good thing that Paul's faith was not based on personal comfort or favorable circumstances. He knew that God was faithful and loved him in spite of the great adversity that he faced.

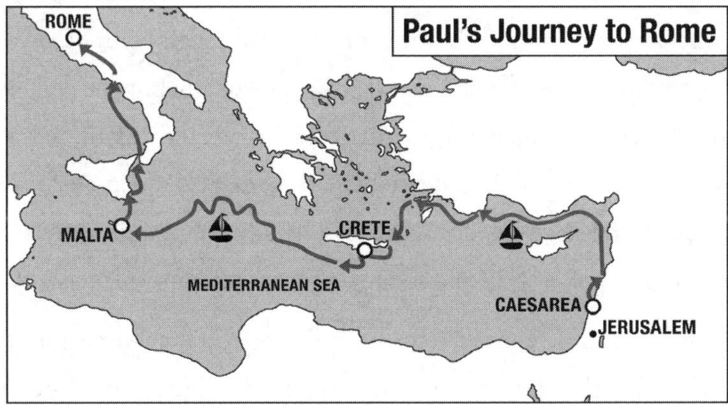

Lessons from Paul's Storm

There are several lessons that we can learn from the stormy situation that Paul survived.

1. Other people can create storms for us. As we've already stated, Paul got into his storm because of the bad decisions and wrong actions of others. Though Paul disagreed with the decision to sail from Crete, he still ended up suffering because of the mistake of others. How often in life does this kind of situation happen?

- Husbands and wives are adversely affected because of bad decisions made by their spouse.
- Children are hurt because of bad decisions and wrong actions of parents.
- Parents suffer because of something their children do.
- A responsible person is damaged by the irresponsibility of another.
- An honest person is hurt by a dishonest person.
- Vulnerable people are hurt by those who abuse power.
- Leaders and groups are hurt by an antagonistic, critical person.

Sometimes the actions of others are overt and directly affect us. Other times, the action is indirect, but the affect is still tangible. In other words, the action might not have been aimed at you personally, but you still feel the consequence. For example, you might go to a store and pay more for your purchases than you ought in order to help the owners compensate for people who shoplift. The store recoups its losses at your expense. Likewise, you pay taxes to support police, jails, and so forth because other people break the law.

2. Another lesson we can learn from Paul's storm is that we've got to keep our heart right. The actions of others can affect us, but we must be careful

not to get into self-pity or develop a victim mentality. Nursing a grudge over the offenses of others can hurt us more than the original transgression ever did. Staying free from unforgiveness, resentment, bitterness, and offense is essential, and we can look to God to help us do what we could not accomplish in our own strength.

Paul's initial perception was that there would be loss of life if they sailed from Crete. When the angel appeared to him, one of the statements made to Paul was, "God has granted you all those who sail with you" (Acts 27:24). This wording—God has granted you—makes me think that Paul had prayed very sincerely and earnestly for the others on board that ship. Paul didn't just pray for his own deliverance, but he actually prayed for the people who put him in that terrible situation. This shows an enormous amount of grace and spiritual maturity on Paul's part.

3. Perseverance is a must if we want to make it through storms. We would be wise to follow Winston Churchill's sage advice: "If you're going through hell, keep going." What beat these travelers down so badly was not simply a storm, but a long, enduring storm. It was the unrelenting nature of the storm that brought them to a state of complete despair. After Paul's visitation from the angel, we read, "Now when the fourteenth night had come, as we were driven up and down in the Adriatic Sea..." (Acts 27:27). I can only imagine that fourteen days on that ship must have felt like fourteen years to those men.

They suffered so long that Luke wrote in Acts 27:20, "It had been many days since we had seen either sun or stars. Wind and waves were battering us unmercifully, and we lost all hope of rescue" (MSG). He went on to describe the condition of those on board, saying that "our appetite for both food and life long gone" (Acts 27:21, MSG). It was against that dismal and hopeless backdrop that Paul arose in Heaven-inspired faith and declared that God's deliverance was coming for them all!

Centuries before Paul's situation, Solomon had noted, "Hope deferred makes the heart sick" (Proverbs 13:12). He also said, "If you faint in the day of adversity, your strength is small" (Proverbs 24:10). If we are to do well in life, we must learn to resist the discouragement that comes when troubles persist.

Legendary football coach Vince Lombardi once said, "Fatigue makes cowards of us all." It can be tempting to become weary and "throw in the towel" if we don't soon experience the circumstances we desire or see results as quickly as want. Hebrews 6:12 admonishes us to "imitate those who through faith and patience inherit the promises." Notice, those who inherit the promises are those who exercise faith *and* patience.

You may not have an angel visit and give you specifics about the outcome of your situation, but the Holy Spirit can minister assurance to you, and He can illuminate certain Bible promises for your encouragement. He will encourage you to "not cast away your confidence, which has great reward" (Hebrews 10:35). Remember: delay is not denial!

Most of us, if we could, would always choose instantaneous answers to our prayers and immediate solutions to our problems. As someone said, "We all want a drive-through breakthrough." A question I've often pondered is why the storm in Mark 4 ended instantly and miraculously, while Paul seemingly had to ride the storm out. But even though Paul's deliverance happened through more of a process (rather than an event), something very notable did happen.

It is worth noting that even Jesus did not make every storm stop immediately. In Matthew 14:25 we see Jesus walking *on* the turbulent waves. Apparently He walked on the waters for some time before the sea grew calm.

I'm not wise enough to know why things don't always happen as quickly as I'd like, but I know that my faith in God must be unconditionally based on the Word of God, and not contingent on whether outcomes occur in a timeframe that I desire. On this subject, the wisdom expressed by an Old Testament prophet has inspired and encouraged many throughout the ages.

> **Though the fig tree may not blossom,**
> **Nor fruit be on the vines;**
> **Though the labor of the olive may fail,**
> **And the fields yield no food;**
> **Though the flock may be cut off from the fold,**
> **And there be no herd in the stalls—**
> **Yet I will rejoice in the LORD,**
> **I will joy in the God of my salvation.**
> **The LORD God is my strength;**
> **He will make my feet like deer's feet,**
> **And He will make me walk on my high hills.**
>
> **Habakkuk 3:17-19**

Paul probably felt for a season that he was not seeing the results he desired, but he kept his heart open, and he saw God come through for him. He got through his storm, and made it to Rome.

Concluding Thought: Paul got into his storm because of the disobedience of others. He got out of his storm through his persevering, enduring faith in God.

Questions for Reflection and Discussion

1. We think of Paul as a man of great faith, and yet he was a man who went through great trials. Do you see a contradiction in this, or is that consistent with your understanding of life?
2. Have you had a situation (or situations) in life where the decisions and actions of others brought a storm into your life? Are you through those storms, still in the midst of them, or a combination of both?
3. If and when you faced a storm because of the decisions and actions of others, were you able to keep a good attitude? Did you struggle with bitterness and resentment? Were you able to forgive the other party and pray for them as Paul did? If so, how?
4. Have you, like Paul, ever faced a storm that just seemed to go on and on? Have you ever experienced what seemed like a long delay in getting through a particular storm? Were you able to maintain your hope and confidence? Did you struggle with weariness due to how long the trial lasted?
5. Have you ever had a hard landing? In other words, have you ever gotten through a situation, but it wasn't a smooth, easy outcome? Were you still able to see God's hand in your rescue even though there was more turbulence than you would have liked?
6. Re-read the Habakkuk 3:17-19 passage. Can you think of a specific time in your life when you identified strongly with those words?

Chapter Five

The Storms Within

When my heart is overwhelmed; Lead me to the rock that is higher than I.

- Psalm 61:2

Key Thought: If you focus only on the external storm, you may be ignoring what could be the most detrimental storm of all: the storm within your own soul.

When adversity comes, our natural tendency is to focus on the external storm. We want relief from the pressure and pain. We just want the winds, the waves, and the danger to stop. It is vital to remember, though, that whenever there is an external storm, there is usually an internal storm as well. The internal storm—what we might refer to as the inner angst or soul turmoil—can be just as detrimental to our lives, if not more so, than the external circumstances.

It may be natural to have an emotional reaction to problems, but it's supernatural to find God's peace, strength, and stability to keep us steady and secure in the midst of trouble. We've examined three storms in the Bible, and we've perhaps alluded in passing to some of the internal storms that accompanied them, but let's focus on the "storms within" more carefully.

Jonah's Internal Storm

It is easy to read the book of Jonah and assume that the only storm he encountered was the one at sea, while he was on the ship. If we look a bit deeper, we realize that that was only the *external* storm; there was another storm that took place within Jonah's own soul. What was the nature of that inner storm?

Jonah had to overcome an internal storm of disobedience before he could move beyond his external problems. Nineveh, where God told Jonah to go preach, was the capital of the Assyrian empire, and the Assyrians and Israelites were bitter enemies. Jonah really did not want the Ninevites to be delivered. Perhaps due to strong nationalistic feelings, he would have preferred to see them destroyed. There was a stubbornness and possibly a prejudice in Jonah that created within him an intense reluctance obey God. As a matter of fact, when his preaching was successful and the Ninevites repented, Jonah was angry that the foretold destruction did not come to pass.

> **But it displeased Jonah exceedingly, and he became angry. So he prayed to the LORD, and said, "Ah, LORD, was not this what I said when I was still in my country? Therefore I fled previously to Tarshish; for I know that You are a gracious and merciful God, slow to anger and abundant in lovingkindness, One who relents from doing harm. Therefore now, O LORD, please take my life from me, for it is better for me to die than to live!"**
>
> **Jonah 4:1-3**

The storm at sea was temporary, but the storm within Jonah was still brewing even as the book closed. Jonah had become obedient, and we give him credit for that. That's what got Jonah out of the fish in the first place. However, Jonah had not become truly willing. Isaiah 1:19 says, "If you are willing and obedient, you shall eat the good of the land." Mere external compliance to an external command is not the same as heartfelt obedience. Jonah preached in Nineveh, but he never allowed his heart to be touched by God's compassion for the people of that place.

God worked His plan *through* Jonah, but was not able to work His plan *in* Jonah. In other words, God accomplished a *transaction* of ministry through Jonah, but we do not see *transformation* happening in Jonah himself. I'm an optimist, and I would like to believe that Jonah's heart eventually softened, but at the end of the book, Jonah was still pouting, fuming, and angry. Jonah was long past the external storm at sea, but the internal storm of unwillingness still churned.

The Disciples' Internal Storm

The disciples' internal storm can be summarized in one word: fear. After Jesus had calmed the external storm, He asked them, "Why are you so fearful? How is it that you have no faith?" (Mark 4:40). Even if Jesus had not identified their problem, we would know that fear was an issue for them based on their initial communication to Him once the boat began filling with water. They said, "Teacher, do You not care that we are perishing?" (Mark 4:38). If you believe that God doesn't care about you or care that you are perishing, that's a pretty good sset-up for fear to work destructively in your life.

When we talk about fear, we're not necessarily talking about full-blown panic. During a lifesaving course I took as a teenager, we had to memorize the following definition: "Panic is the sudden, overwhelming, unreasoning fear which overtakes a person in the face of real or imagined danger." While some may be panicked, others are simply carrying what we might call a seed of fear, a low-grade condition that irritates and distracts, and keeps them from truly enjoying life. Many people have learned to put on a happy face and act like everything's all right when, in reality, they are dealing with worry, anxiety, and fear.

Arthur Somers Roche said, "Worry is a thin stream of fear trickling through the mind. If encouraged, it cuts a channel into which all other thoughts are drained." Some people have worry or fear so integrated into their identity that they don't realize they're a slave to it. To them, that's just the way they are. That's the way they've always thought. That's the way they've always believed. That's the way they've always felt.

Fear can be identified and fueled through certain underlying beliefs:

- I don't feel good enough.
- I don't measure up.
- I won't have enough; I will always lack.
- I just have this pervasive sense that something bad is going to happen.
- I won't succeed; I am doomed to failure.
- Others will reject me and disapprove of me.

Fear needs to be identified, recognized, and eradicated! John, one of the disciples on board the boat in Mark 4, later wrote, "There is no fear in love; but perfect love casts out fear, because fear involves torment. But he who fears has not been made perfect in love. We love Him because He first loved us" (1 John 4:18-19). One of the best ways to stay free from fear is to keep ourselves saturated with the knowledge of how much God loves us.

And because He loves us, He is totally committed to us. His love for us is revealed in the promise He made to never leave or forsake us (see Hebrews 13:5-6).

One way to combat fear is to arm ourselves with the Word of God! Here are just a few of the many Scriptures that we can meditate upon and confess.

> **Do not be afraid, nor be dismayed; be strong and of good courage...**
>
> **Joshua 10:25**

> **The LORD is my light and my salvation;**
> **Whom shall I fear?**
> **The LORD is the strength of my life;**
> **Of whom shall I be afraid?**
> **When the wicked came against me**
> **To eat up my flesh,**
> **My enemies and foes,**
> **They stumbled and fell.**
> **Though an army may encamp against me,**
> **My heart shall not fear;**
> **Though war may rise against me,**
> **In this I will be confident.**
>
> **Psalm 27:1-3**

> **God is our refuge and strength,**
> **A very present help in trouble.**
> **Therefore we will not fear,**
> **Even though the earth be removed,**
> **And though the mountains be carried into the midst of the sea.**
>
> **Psalm 46:1-2**

You will keep him in perfect peace, whose mind is stayed on You, because he trusts in You.

Isaiah 26:3

Fear not, for I am with you; Be not dismayed, for I am your God. I will strengthen you, yes, I will help you, I will uphold you with My righteous right hand.

Isaiah 41:10

In righteousness you shall be established; You shall be far from oppression, for you shall not fear; And from terror, for it shall not come near you.

Isaiah 54:14

Do not be afraid; only believe.

Mark 5:36

Peace I leave with you, My peace I give to you; not as the world gives do I give to you. Let not your heart be troubled, neither let it be afraid.

John 14:27

For God has not given us a spirit of fear, but of power and of love and of a sound mind.

2 Timothy 1:7

Determine that you will not live under the tyranny of fear. Resolve not to be paralyzed by worry or dread. Let God's love, acceptance, and promises be very real to you, and allow His Word to live big in your heart. After the disciples were filled with the Holy Spirit, they demonstrated fearlessness and boldness in the face of severe threats and intense persecution (read Acts 4). They ultimately conquered the internal storm of fear!

Paul's Internal Storm

The first words out of the angel's mouth when he appeared to Paul were, "Do not be afraid, Paul..." (Acts 27:24). It's easy to understand, based on the circumstances he was encountering, that Paul would have been dealing with fear; and this wouldn't have been the only time that Paul had dealt with it.

> **When we came to Macedonia, our bodies had no rest, but we were troubled on every side. Outside were conflicts, inside were fears. Nevertheless God, who comforts the downcast, comforted us by the coming of Titus.**
>
> **2 Corinthians 7:5-6**

It's interesting to me that on the ship, God sent Paul an angel to comfort him. In Macedonia, God sent Paul a friend—Titus. God is committed to comforting us when we are down, but He may do it in different ways at different times. Paul said that God "comforts us in all our tribulation, that we may be able to comfort those who are in any trouble, with the comfort with which we ourselves are comforted by God" (2 Corinthians 1:4).

Another inner storm that Paul faced during the course of his ministry was despair. In Second Corinthians 1:8, Paul said, "...we do not want you to be ignorant, brethren, of our trouble which came to us in Asia: that we were burdened beyond measure, above strength, so that we despaired even of life." Does it shock you to realize that such a great man of God faced such negative emotions? Have you ever felt that if you had enough faith or were spiritual enough, you wouldn't experience such things? Don't let yourself be condemned if you face these emotions; having emotions to deal with doesn't mean that you're unspiritual or lack faith. It simply means that you're human. Look to God, though, and allow Him to comfort you, encourage you, and strengthen you.

In addition to dealing with fear and despair, Paul could have gotten very bitter and resentful toward the people whose bad decisions put him in that terrible situation. Instead, it appears that he prayed for them. As we saw previously, part of the angel's message to Paul was, "God has granted you all those who sail with you" (Acts 27:24). This seems to imply that Paul had been interceding on their behalf. How tempting, though, it would have been for Paul to adopt a victim mentality. How easily he could have slipped into self-pity. Paul ultimately overcame the external storm because he first overcame the storm within.

To not forgive those who have hurt you can keep an internal storm brewing in your soul, even if the external storm has already passed. I agree with Augustine, who said, "If you are suffering from a bad man's injustice, forgive him lest there be two bad men."

In advocating forgiveness toward those who hurt us, I am not promoting putting ourselves (or keeping ourselves) in a position where we are *unnecessarily* vulnerable. Keep in mind that Paul was a prisoner and did not have the power to choose whether that ship set sail. However, in many situations in life, we do have a choice to keep ourselves out of unwise, high-risk situations where our exposure to unnecessary pain is increased.

For example, if your financial situation is damaged because you co-signed for someone—made yourself liable for her debts—*you* put yourself in that situation. You probably assumed that other person would be responsible toward her obligations, but you could have avoided that pain had you not agreed to the deal. Consider the wisdom Solomon shared with those who have created unnecessary vulnerability for themselves:

My child, if you have put up security for a friend's debt
or agreed to guarantee the debt of a stranger—
if you have trapped yourself by your agreement
and are caught by what you said—
follow my advice and save yourself,
for you have placed yourself at your friend's mercy.
Now swallow your pride;
go and beg to have your name erased.
Don't put it off; do it now!
Don't rest until you do.
Save yourself like a gazelle escaping from a hunter,
like a bird fleeing from a net.

Proverbs 6:1-5 (NLT)

I believe we should forgive when someone has hurt us, but I'm also in favor of our walking in common sense and biblical sense and therefore not setting ourselves up to be hurt unnecessarily.

Another temptation Paul could have faced was that of becoming bitter and angry at God. Can you imagine Paul—in the midst of that terrible storm—saying, "God, I've served you all these years, and this is the thanks I get? If You don't love me more than this, then I'm not going to serve You anymore!" Paul realized that he could not interpret the love or goodness of God based on his circumstances. Paul tenaciously clung to God like Abraham, who, "contrary to hope, in hope believed" (Romans 4:18).

The Internal Storms of David

Throughout Scripture, many others experienced storms or difficult seasons as well. God said that David was "a man after My own heart" (Acts 13:22), and yet David faced many storms, both external and internal. These internal storms are often described in vivid detail throughout the Book of Psalms. Consider some of these descriptions that reveal how David responded to the anguish he sometimes experienced in his soul.

> **Why are you cast down, O my soul? And why are you disquieted within me? Hope in God; for I shall yet praise Him, the help of my countenance and my God.**
>
> **Psalm 42:11**

> **In the multitude of my anxieties within me, Your comforts delight my soul.**
>
> **Psalm 94:19**

> **Return to your rest, O my soul, for the LORD has dealt bountifully with you.**
>
> **Psalm 116:7**

> **I remembered Your judgments of old, O LORD, and have comforted myself.**
>
> **Psalm 119:52**

> **Surely I have calmed and quieted my soul, like a weaned child with his mother; like a weaned child is my soul within me.**
>
> **Psalm 131:2**

David had multiple opportunities to seek peace within, and he did not deny the existence of turmoil when it was present. What did he do? He looked to God and actively ministered to himself by speaking encouraging and comforting words to himself, reminding himself that God was good and faithful and worthy to be trusted.

One of the most vivid examples of this is found in First Samuel 30, when David and his men experienced a disastrous setback. While they were out on a military expedition, an enemy army stole their wives, children, and possessions. After weeping, David's men decided take out their grief and anger by killing him. David's response is amazing!

> **David was greatly distressed, for the men spoke of stoning him because the souls of them all were bitterly grieved, each man for his sons and daughters. But David encouraged and strengthened himself in the Lord his God.**
>
> **1 Samuel 30:6 (AMP)**

David was facing a major external storm and a major internal storm, but his faith in God lifted him above them both. When you find yourself facing adverse circumstances, don't simply fixate on finding relief from the circumstances, but make sure you strengthen yourself in the Lord your God and get established in His peace—the safest place to ride out any kind of storm.

Concluding Thought: If you focus only on the external storm, you may be ignoring what could be the most detrimental storm of all: the storm within your own soul.

Questions for Reflection and Discussion

1. Have you ever gotten caught up in an internal storm due to an external storm you encountered? What were the characteristics of your internal storm, and how did you deal with it?

3. Mark Twain said, "I've had a lot of worries in my life, most of which never happened." Have you ever had an internal storm in anticipation of an external storm that never materialized? How did you feel when the external storm never happened and you realized how much energy you'd spent dealing with an internal storm based on something that never even developed?

3. Have you, like Jonah, ever been reluctant to do the will of God? Have you ever had to deal with stubbornness like Jonah did? Have you ever been obedient without being willing? How did you become both willing *and* obedient?

4. We saw where the disciples moved from fear during one phase of their lives to boldness in another period. Can you relate to that kind of growth? How did God lead you in that journey?

5. Paul could have faced an inner storm of resentment and unforgiveness toward those who created problems in his life. He also described times when he dealt with fear and despair. Does it help you to realize that being spiritual doesn't mean living problem-free, but that spirituality is revealed by how you respond to life's problems? How have you dealt with such issues in your own life?

6. Review the scriptures in which David responded to the anguish that he sometimes experienced in his soul. Can you relate to how he trusted God and encouraged himself? Can you relate to the idea of encouraging yourself in the Lord?

Chapter Six

It's About the Destination

"Obstacles are those frightful things you see when you take your eyes off the goal."

- Henry Ford

Key Thought: Instead of focusing on the storms, set your heart on your destination. Jonah made it to Nineveh; the disciples made it to the other side; and Paul made it to Rome. Fasten your gaze and direct your attention to your goals and destiny, not the storms and obstacles.

Even though this book deals with overcoming and moving beyond storms, we must realize that life involves much more than dealing with problems and surviving storms. Life is not merely about survival, and it's about more than success. Life is about finding significance. Survival is getting what I need. Success (at least as the world defines it) is getting what I want. Significance, though, is giving what I can give; significance is measured by the difference I make in the lives of others.

Jonah's Destination

God's ultimate purpose for Jonah was not just to get him out of the storm or out of the fish; it was to get him to Nineveh so that the city could receive God's forgiveness. Jonah 3:5 says, "The people of Nineveh believed God's message, and from the greatest to the least, they declared a fast and put on burlap to show their sorrow" (NLT). Even the king and his nobles declared, "...everyone must pray earnestly to God. They must turn from their evil ways and stop all their violence" (Jonah 3:8, NLT). The people were spared through repentance and faith in God, and that's what Jonah's assignment was all about.

The Destination of Jesus and the Disciples

Likewise, the purpose of the journey to the other side of the Sea of Galilee was not to simply get Jesus and the disciples through a storm, but to liberate and minister deliverance to a desperate man who had lived a life of torment and anguish.

> **And when He had come out of the boat, immediately there met Him out of the tombs a man with an unclean spirit, who had his dwelling among the tombs; and no one could bind him, not even with chains, because he had often been bound with shackles and chains. And the chains had been pulled apart by him, and the shackles broken in pieces; neither could anyone tame him. And always, night and day, he was in the mountains and in the tombs, crying out and cutting himself with stones.**
>
> **Mark 5:2-5**

After Jesus ministered healing and deliverance to this man we read that the man "was sitting there fully clothed and perfectly sane"

Enjoy the Journey?

We're often told to "enjoy the journey," and I agree completely. It's easier to enjoy a journey, however, if we have at least somewhat of an idea of where we're headed. Yogi Berra, who was known for making zany, paradoxical statements said, "You've got to be very careful if you don't know where you're going, because you might not get there." Author Lewis Carroll said, "If you don't know where you're going, any road will get you there."

None of us know everything. Even Paul acknowledged that now we only know and see in part (1 Corinthians 13:9-12). But that's okay; only God is omniscient. We should be growing in the knowledge of His will, and our lives will be enriched as we obtain a clearer vision of who God has called us to be and what God has called us to do. We'll travel more effectively if we have insight from God as to where we're heading.

The road we travel won't always be smooth, but when we know our destination and we know that God is always with us, we can continue the journey with confidence. Like all of us, David was on a journey through life and part of that journey involved a stormy season that he referred to as "the valley of the shadow of death."

> **Yea, though I walk through the valley of the shadow of death,**
> **I will fear no evil;**
> **For You are with me;**
> **Your rod and Your staff, they comfort me.**
>
> **Psalm 23:4**

Notice that David had a certain perspective on passing through that dark season. He said, "Yea, though I walk through...." David was not settling down or setting up camp in the valley of the shadow of death; he was passing *through*. The negative aspect of the journey was temporary, but

David was persuaded that goodness and mercy would follow him all the days of his life and that he would dwell in the house of the Lord forever (Psalm 23:6).

Yes, enjoy the journey as much as you can, but never lose sight of your goal! The heroes of faith described in Hebrews chapter 11 all received a good testimony from Heaven because of their unwavering commitment to God and His plan.

> **These all died in faith, not having received the promises, but having seen them afar off were assured of them, embraced them and confessed that they were strangers and pilgrims on the earth. For those who say such things declare plainly that they seek a homeland. And truly if they had called to mind that country from which they had come out, they would have had opportunity to return. But now they desire a better, that is, a heavenly country. Therefore God is not ashamed to be called their God, for He has prepared a city for them.**
>
> **Hebrews 11:13-16**

Each of these believers ran their assigned course in a great relay race, but the complete fulfillment of God's larger plan was many generations away from them. Still, they envisioned and anticipated a great future where God's plan would be fully realized.

Earthly and Eternal Destinations

We must realize that when it comes to this life on earth, we're all just passing through. Speaking of our journey, Peter said that we are "sojourners and pilgrims" (1 Peter 2:11). The NLT says that we are "temporary residents and foreigners." At the end of his earthly journey, Paul said, "Finally, there is laid up for me the crown of righteousness, which the Lord, the righteous Judge, will give to me on that Day, and not to me only but also to all who have loved His appearing" (2 Timothy 4:8). This temporal life isn't the end; eternity with Christ awaits us.

In First Corinthians 15:19, Paul said, "If in this life only we have hope in Christ, we are of all men most miserable" (KJV). The Message Version renders this, "If all we get out of Christ is a little inspiration for a few short years, we're a pretty sorry lot." Keep Heaven in mind! Heaven is not a cop-out for people who don't want to be responsible in this life. It is the abode of God, and it is where the righteous will go when this life is over.

Fulfill your destiny here on earth. Enjoy the journey as you seek to become and do all that God has for you. Don't let the storms of life distract you from your purpose. Remember the words made famous in John Newton's timeless hymn "Amazing Grace":

Through many dangers, toils and snares,
I have already come;
'Tis grace hath brought me safe thus far,
and grace will lead me home.

Let God's grace lead you through the storms of life—through the dangers, toils, and snares—and into your earthly and eternal destinations.

Concluding Thought: Instead of focusing on the storms, set your heart on your destination. Jonah made it to Nineveh; the disciples made it to the other side; and Paul made it to Rome. Fasten your gaze and direct your attention to your goals and destiny, not the storms and obstacles.

Questions for Reflection and Discussion

1. What is your most frequent mindset—survival, success, or significance? If your mindset is not where you'd like it to be, what do you need to do to help move it in the right direction?
2. Having a clear picture of one's destination seems to be a key factor in being able to persevere through storms. How clear are your goals for yourself, and are you confident that your goals are consistent with God's plan for your life?
3. Do you tend to get preoccupied by the storms you encounter? Do the storms get you disoriented, so to speak, causing you to lose sight of your purpose and goals? What do you do to get refocused? How do you keep the storm from completely distracting you?
4. Which of the four quotes from the "Traits of Achievers" section was the most meaningful to you? Why was this quote especially meaningful?
5. How are you doing when it comes to enjoying your journey? Have you been able to keep your joy as you navigate through the storms of life?
6. Consider the words of John Newton's hymn, "Amazing Grace." To what extent has God's grace has been involved in leading you through the storms of life? How have you experienced God's grace and what does His grace mean to you?

Chapter Seven

The Four-Wheel Drive Christian

"If you only have a hammer, you tend to see every problem as a nail."
- Abraham Maslow

Key Thought: Don't be a one-dimensional believer. Utilize as many of the tools and resources that God has given you in order to live an effective and victorious Christian life.

Lisa and I have lived in Oklahoma since our marriage in 1979. As a result, we've not had much need for a four-wheel drive vehicle. During one ten-month period, though, we lived in Colorado and that locale gave us an entirely different perspective on driving. Several winter days we drove very tentatively (and prayerfully) in heavy snow, while confident drivers with four-wheel drive blew right past us. Their traction and grip on the road was far superior to ours in difficult conditions, and they weren't slipping or sliding the way we were.

What was the difference? They had all four tires working for them, and we didn't!

Spiritually speaking, God never intended for us to try to get through all of the challenges and difficulties of life with only one tire providing traction. In other words, we're not designed to go through life relying on and implementing only one aspect of God's Word. We are to look at Scripture from an integrated perspective, not from an isolated perspective. Notice that Jesus said that man shall live "by every word that proceeds from the mouth of God" (Matthew 4:4), not merely by selected or isolated words of God.

Let's illustrate this. The Apostle James demonstrated how various spiritual forces can and should work together cooperatively, especially in hard times.

> **My brethren, count it all joy when you fall into various trials, knowing that the testing of your faith produces patience. But let patience have its perfect work, that you may be perfect and complete, lacking nothing. If any of you lacks wisdom, let him ask of God, who gives to all liberally and without reproach, and it will be given to him.**
>
> **James 1:2-5**

We might say that James was encouraging every believer to be a "four-wheel drive Christian." In this passage, the four wheels he identifies are joy, faith, patience, and wisdom. Martin Luther said, "We are saved by faith alone, but the faith that saves never stands alone." These spiritual forces were designed by God to be complimentary and to work in collaboration with each other.

Think about those four traits for a moment: joy, faith, patience, and wisdom. Can you imagine how difficult it would be to operate in only one of these areas, while giving no place to the others? For example, think how hard it would be to stand in faith and trust God, if you had no joy, were completely impatient, and lacked wisdom. Faith is wonderful and essential, but we need to embrace all of the "cooperating powers" that God designed to work together for our benefit.

Joy gives buoyancy, vibrancy, and "lift" to our lives. Joy is related to cheerfulness, gladness, and rejoicing. According to Nehemiah 8:10, "...the joy of the LORD is your strength." Acknowledging the significance of joy in conjunction with faith, Paul told the Philippians that he desired to, "...help all of you grow and experience the joy of your faith" (Philippians 1:25, NLT). It is important to understand that the spiritual force of joy is not based on circumstances. Psalm 16:11 says, "In Your presence is fullness of joy." Proverbs 17:22 says, "A joyful heart is good medicine" (ESV). Jesus said, "These things I have spoken to you, that My joy may remain in you, and that your joy may be full" (John 15:11).

Speaking of the great challenges and adversity he knew he would face, Paul said, "But none of these things move me; nor do I count my life dear to myself, so that I may finish my race with joy..." (Acts 20:24). God's love was clearly a prime motivator in what Jesus did for humanity, but we also find in Scripture that joy was a major impetus for Him as well. We read of the Savior: "...because of the joy that was waiting for him, he thought nothing of the disgrace of dying on the cross, and he is now seated at the right-hand side of God's throne" (Hebrews 12:2, GNB).

James' statement to "count it all joy when you fall into various trials" is probably one of the most unnatural, counter-intuitive directives in the Bible. Note that James did not say "if" you fall into various trials, he said "when." James was realistic and wanted his readers to know that certain challenges in life are inevitable. How we respond to them is what really matters!

We need to remain optimistic, even in bad situations. I remember hearing a story about a behavioral psychologist who was doing an experiment to see how children handled difficult circumstances. A young boy was led into a small room containing a considerable amount of horse manure. Instead of reacting negatively with whining and crying, the boy became excited and happy, and actually began playfully digging around in the manure. When the psychologist asked him why he was so happy, the little boy joyfully replied, "With all this manure, there just has to be a pony in here somewhere!" I don't know how true that story is, but what an optimistic attitude that boy had!

When we fall into various trials, our natural reaction is to complain, worry, and feel sorry for ourselves. When we have God's perspective on the matter, we truly can count it joy because we have a confident expectation that God is working in our lives to bring us out victoriously on the other side. The problems we encounter simply present us with a wonderful opportunity to see God work on our behalf!

Consider a championship team. When they hear they're going to be tested by an opponent, they don't worry and become fearful. Because they are champions, they believe they can beat the other team. They focus their energies and face their opponent with an optimism that expresses their belief: "This is just another opportunity to win!"

In addition to joy, we must have faith. **Faith** is trusting God's character and His Word. It speaks of strong reliance upon, stalwart confidence in, and a firm adherence to who God is and what He has said. The Bible says that "faith comes by hearing, and hearing by the word of God" (Romans 10:17).

- We *live* by faith (Romans 1:17).

- We are *justified* by faith (Romans 3:28).
- We *stand* by faith (2 Corinthians 1:24).
- We *walk* by faith (2 Corinthians 5:7).
- We are *saved* by faith (Ephesians 2:8).

According to the Bible, so much of how we live our life is dependent upon faith. So what is faith? D.L. Moody said, "The best definition I can find of faith is the dependence upon the veracity of another. The Bible definition in the 11th chapter of Hebrews is, 'Faith is the substance of things hoped for, the evidence of things not seen.' In other words, faith says amen to everything that God says. Faith takes God without any ifs. If God says it, Faith says I believe it; Faith says amen to it."[5] In a similar vein, Martin Luther once said, "Faith is the 'yes' of the heart."

One of the great principles of Scripture is that of yielding your self-life and allowing God to live through you. Don't think that you are supposed to fight every battle and conquer every adversity in your own strength. A huge part of faith is simply relying upon God. I love what Psalm 57:2 says: "I will cry out to God Most High, to God who performs all things for me." The HCSB says, "I call to God Most High, to God who fulfills His purpose for me." There are times when God says, "The battle is not yours, but God's," and, "Stand still and see the salvation of the LORD" (2 Chronicles 20:15,17).

Hebrews 11:6 says that "without faith it is impossible to please Him, for he who comes to God must believe that He is, and that He is a rewarder of those who diligently seek Him." Don't get down on yourself if you feel like you don't have strong faith. Don't look to yourself at all. Look to God and His Word; that's where faith comes from. Faith won't grow if you

[5] D.L. Moody, *To All People: Glad Tidings Comprising Sermons, Bible Readings, Temperance Addresses, and Prayer-Meeting Talks* (New York: Treat, 1877), 170.

are focused on yourself—look to Jesus, and let Him be the Author and Finisher of your faith (Hebrews 12:2).

There are many different ways that faith works in our life, and various expressions it takes as it helps us. Scripture speaks of:

- The *spirit* of faith (2 Corinthians 4:13)
- The *shield* of faith (Ephesians 6:16)
- The *joy* of faith (Philippians 1:25)
- The *breastplate* of faith (1 Thessalonians 5:8)
- The *work* of faith (2 Thessalonians 2:11)
- The *words* of faith (1 Timothy 4:6)
- The *fight* of faith (1 Timothy 6:12)
- The *assurance* of faith (Hebrews 10:22)
- The *prayer* of faith (James 5:15).

Your faith will be challenged. The Apostle Peter said to Christians who were facing persecution, "So be truly glad. There is wonderful joy ahead, even though you have to endure many trials for a little while. These trials will show that your faith is genuine. It is being tested as fire tests and purifies gold—though your faith is far more precious than mere gold. So when your faith remains strong through many trials, it will bring you much praise and glory and honor on the day when Jesus Christ is revealed to the whole world" (1 Peter 1:6-7, NLT). Continue in faith even while it is being tested; keep your eyes on Jesus, and your faith will be tried and true.

Smith Wigglesworth said, "Great faith is the product of great fights. Great testimonies are the outcome of great tests. Great triumphs can only come out of great trials." Faith in God will cause you to see trials as stepping-stones, not tombstones— as building blocks, not stumbling blocks.

Faith enables you to see the opportunity in each obstacle. As Hudson Taylor said, "All our difficulties are only platforms for the manifestations of His grace, power and love."

Patience (endurance) is what gives staying power to our faith. We'd all love it if every desired result was instantaneous, but we know that there is often a process involved. I believe that's why Hebrews 6:12 tells us that it's through "faith and patience" that we inherit the promises. Faith is our trusting God, and patience is our unwavering tenacity in doing so.

James says that "...the testing of your faith produces patience. But let patience have its perfect work, that you may be perfect and complete, lacking nothing" (James 1:3-4). Paul says something similar in Romans 5:3-4, "...we also glory in tribulations, knowing that tribulation produces perseverance; and perseverance, character; and character, hope." Some people mistakenly believe that trials will automatically make them more refined, spiritual people. That's not true. Paul was talking specifically to people who were standing in grace and rejoicing in the hope of the glory of God.

It's important to understand that trials—in and of themselves—don't make you strong spiritually any more than weights (in and of themselves) make you strong physically. It's what you do against the weights—lifting them, using them to walk or exercise—that builds your physical muscles. And it's what you do in the midst of trials—trusting God, rejoicing, persevering, and so forth—that develops your spiritual strength.

We've probably all known people who went through trials and tribulations and became bitter, disheartened, and disillusioned about life. The trials certainly didn't make them better people. It's how we *respond* to adversity—not the trial itself—that will determine whether we become bitter or better, whether we shrivel or grow.

That word "patience" which James uses is not a passive word; it does not imply inactivity or refer to miserably tolerating a situation. When you encounter trials, don't just surrender and become resigned and apathetic; that's not patience. Rather, this word refers to a "persevering endurance and continuance."[6] One commentary says patience suggests "...endurance or stamina. It also includes staying power that believers can have because they trust their God. Tested faith becomes spiritually tough and rugged."[7] Yet another commentary says this word means "steadfastness or endurance in the face of difficulties."[8] Kenneth Wuest translates the Greek word as "a patience which bears up and does not lose heart or courage under trials."[9]

Referring to the Greek word translated "patience," William Barclay says, "*Hupomonē* is not simply the ability to bear things; it is the ability to turn them to greatness and to glory. The thing which amazed the heathen in the centuries of persecution was that the martyrs did not die grimly, they died singing. One smiled in the flames; they asked him what he found to smile at there. 'I saw the glory of God,' he said, 'and was glad.' *Hupomonē* is the quality which makes a man able, not simply to suffer things, but to vanquish them. The effect of testing rightly borne is strength to bear still more and to conquer in still harder battles."[10] Proverbs 24:10 says, "If you faint in the day of adversity, your strength is small." Real faith never runs up the white flag of surrender at the first sign of trouble. Faith comes out swinging! Patience (or endurance) bolsters your faith, enabling you

---

[6] R. Jamieson,, A. R. Fausset, & D. Brown, *Commentary Critical and Explanatory on the Whole Bible* James 1:3 (Oak Harbor, WA: Logos Research Systems, Inc., 1997).

[7] T. D. Lea, *Holman New Testament Commentary, Vol. 10: Hebrews, James* (Nashville, TN: Broadman & Holman Publishers, 1999), 258.

[8] J. F. Walvoord,, R. B. Zuck, & Dallas Theological Seminary, *The Bible Knowledge Commentary: An Exposition of the Scriptures* James 1:3 (Wheaton, IL: Victor Books, 1985).

[9] K.S. Wuest, *The New Testament: An Expanded Translation* James 1:1–4 (Grand Rapids, MI: Eerdmans, 1961).

[10] W. Barclay, editor, *The Letters of James and Peter: The Daily Study Bible Series* (Philadelphia: Westminster John Knox Press, 1976), 43.

to respond to challenges with an attitude that boldly declares, "I will not quit!"

We've studied what is involved with joy, faith, and patience, but what about the wisdom that James mentions?

> **My brethren, count it all *joy* when you fall into various trials, knowing that the testing of your *faith* produces *patience*. But let patience have its perfect work, that you may be perfect and complete, lacking nothing. If any of you lacks *wisdom*, let him ask of God, who gives to all liberally and without reproach, and it will be given to him.**
>
> **James 1:2-5 (emphasis mine)**

Wisdom is divine insight that enables us to make accurate and precise application of our faith. Some people say they trust God, but their very words, attitudes, and actions (or lack thereof) undermine their faith and prevent them from achieving their desired results. Because of a lack of wisdom, they sabotage their potential success.

Let's look at a hypothetical situation as an example. Zach says he is trusting God for increased financial provision, and he hopes he will receive promotions and raises at his place of employment. He even has joy because of his confidence. However, Zach is not punctual at work, is late completing assignments, and has trouble getting along with other employees. He fails to realize that because he doesn't walk in wisdom, he is actually undermining that for which he is praying. It is not that God is unable or unwilling to bless Zach, but because Zack lacks wisdom or chooses not to apply it, he is sabotaging the very results he's asking God to bring to pass.

The Book of Proverbs is known as the book of wisdom, and it contains many descriptions of the benefits of the wisdom of God's Word.

- Wisdom causes you to "dwell safely" and "be secure, without fear of evil" (Proverbs 1:33).
- Because of wisdom, "discretion will preserve you" and "understanding will keep you" (Proverbs 2:11).
- Wisdom enables you to "walk in the way of goodness, and keep to the paths of righteousness" (Proverbs 2:20).
- When you receive wisdom's influence, "length of days and long life and peace" will be added to you (Proverbs 3:2).
- Wisdom causes you to "find favor and high esteem in the sight of God and man" (Proverbs 3:4).
- Wisdom causes you to fear God and depart from evil, which will be, "health to your flesh, and strength to your bones" (Proverbs 3:8).
- Following wisdom means "your barns will be filled with plenty, and your vats will overflow with new wine" (Proverbs 3:10).
- When you walk in the ways of wisdom, you discover that "length of days is in her right hand, in her left hand riches and honor. Her ways are ways of pleasantness, and all her paths are peace" (Proverbs 3:16-17).
- Wisdom enables you to "walk safely in your way, and your foot will not stumble" (Proverbs 3:23).
- Wisdom "will promote you" and "bring you honor" (Proverbs 4:8).
- Wisdom causes "the years of your life (to) be many" (Proverbs 4:10).

- Through wisdom "your days will be multiplied, and years of life will be added to you" (Proverbs 9:11).

Those are some pretty amazing benefits of wisdom, don't you think? And wisdom is ours for the asking! When I consider the statement by James —"If any of you lacks wisdom, let him ask of God... and it will be given to him"—it makes me extremely grateful that wisdom is available to us. And remember, James was talking especially to people who were in the midst of various trials. Perhaps James was thinking of people who were walking in all the joy, faith, and patience that they had, but who still needed insight to enable them to successfully navigate their storms.

God ordained that we be more than one-dimensional believers; He wants us to be four-wheel drive Christians! We've looked at joy, faith, patience, and wisdom, but in reality, these are only a few of the many attributes that God wants functioning in our lives. We have the privilege of walking in love, praying, serving, and enjoying fellowship with other believers. All of these have great benefits for our lives. Paul and Peter both promoted this cooperative, collaborative approach to the Christian life.

> **Now may the God of hope fill you with all joy and peace in believing, that you may abound in hope by the power of the Holy Spirit.**
>
> **Romans 15:13**

> **...giving all diligence, add to your faith virtue, to virtue knowledge, to knowledge self-control, to self-control perseverance, to perseverance godliness, to godliness brotherly kindness, and to brotherly kindness love. For if these things are yours and abound, you will be neither barren nor unfruitful in the knowledge of our Lord Jesus Christ.**
>
> **2 Peter 1:5-8**

There are several ways we can look at these amazing principles. We could call them "the cooperating powers of God." We could call this concept "the faith team." Or we can simply aspire to be "four-wheel drive Christians" who get good traction and are able to keep moving forward even in turbulent times. Why? Because we're continuing to experience positive momentum in our lives from all the wonderful things that God has invested in us, and we are able to keep moving forward through the storms of life.

Concluding Thought: Don't be a one-dimensional believer. Utilize as many of the tools and resources that God has given you in order to live an effective and victorious Christian life.

Questions for Reflection and Discussion

1. How complete is your understanding of the diverse spiritual resources that God has made available to you? Are you accessing and cultivating these various spiritual attributes in your life? Is there a specific area where you feel you're especially strong? Is there an area where you believe you need significant growth?
2. What is the level of joy in your life? Are you experiencing its strength, vibrancy, buoyancy, and boost in your life? If your joy level seems down, would David's prayer, "Restore to me the joy of Your salvation" (Psalm 51:12) be applicable or helpful?
3. What do you think of Smith Wigglesworth's quote: "Great faith is the product of great fights. Great testimonies are the

outcome of great tests. Great triumphs can only come out of great trials"? Have you experienced the truth of these statements in your own life? How?

4. In the past, what did you think about the role of patience? Have you seen it as something passive or active? Based on the information given in this chapter, how is your patience when you face adversity? Do you operate in a persevering endurance and exhibit spiritual stamina? Is your faith spiritually tough? Do you have a steadfast patience that bears up under hardship and does not lose heart or courage under trials?

5. Explain why trials in and of themselves don't make you a more spiritual person. Have you ever known of someone who, because of the way they responded to problems, actually declined in their spiritual life?

6. Have you ever created or prolonged a storm because of a lack of wisdom on your part? Have you ever recognized the need for wisdom and made it a point to pursue wisdom? Are there specific ways your life has gone better because you embraced God's wisdom in your life and used it in your decision-making?

Chapter Eight

Can I Avoid at Least *Some* Problems?

When you walk, your steps will not be hindered, And when you run, you will not stumble.

Proverbs 4:12

Key Thought: We can't control everything in the universe, but we have a significant amount of influence on many things we experience in life. God makes it clear in His Word that we have choices to make, and that our choices have consequences.

When I first began thinking about this chapter, I was mindful of the many wise and insightful decisions we can make that will help us have a better life and help prevent certain types of problems. However, we need to make sure that we're truly leaning into life, and not just trying to avoid problems. A dread of potential adversity can be more detrimental to our lives than the problem would actually be if we ever encountered it. Can you relate to what Mark Twain meant when he quipped, "I have been through some terrible things in my life, some of which actually happened"?

We can be so fearful of problems that in a state of hyper-vigilance, we anxiously and continuously scan the horizon to detect any potential threats to our security. The problem with such an obsession is that it does not allow us to enjoy life or those around us. I don't want to live life being fearful of failure, fearful of making mistakes, fearful of problems. I want to be intelligent and prudent in life, but I don't want to operate in hyper-cautious, debilitating, anxiety-based avoidance. That would be an impoverishing way to live.

Someone once wrote a rhyme about a man who lived this kind of "life":

There was a very cautious man
Who never risked, or tried.
He never hoped, he never failed;
He never laughed or cried.
And when he one day passed away,
His insurance was denied,
For since he never really lived
They claim he never died!

The rhyme is intended to be humorous but still make a serious point. Given the choice, I much prefer the approach to life that is reflected in what Helen Keller said: "Security is mostly a superstition. It does not exist in nature, nor do the children of men as a whole experience it. Avoiding danger is no safer in the long run than outright exposure. Life is either a daring adventure or nothing." Consider these other insights:

- "The person who gets the farthest is generally the one who is willing to do and dare. The sure-thing boat never gets far from shore."

  - Dale Carnegie

- "If you can find a path with no obstacles, it probably doesn't lead anywhere."

  Frank A. Clark

- "Problems are the price you pay for progress."

  - Branch Rickey

- "Far better it is to dare mighty things, to win glorious triumphs, even though checkered by failure, than to take rank with those poor spirits who neither enjoy much nor suffer much, because they live in the great twilight that knows not victory nor defeat."

  - Theodore Roosevelt

These quotes indicate a truth about life: the life worth living is never without obstacles. There is great liberation in living life boldly and with a sense of adventure, knowing that God is with you and even if you fall, He'll be right there to pick you up. It's better to fail while engaging in life and endeavoring to do something for God, than to succeed at doing nothing. I have no intention of taking reckless, foolish risks, but I do want to live boldly, confidently, and fully.

Having said this, let's go back to our original question: Can we avoid at least some problems in life? We certainly can. Some problems are unavoidable, but for the problems that can be avoided—let's learn how to avoid them!

"What a Friend We Have in Jesus" is a classic hymn whose lyrics were penned by Joseph M. Scriven. In the lyrics, we see an interesting concept.

What a friend we have in Jesus,
All our sins and griefs to bear!
What a privilege to carry
Everything to God in prayer!
Oh, what peace we often forfeit,
Oh, what needless pain we bear,
All because we do not carry
Everything to God in prayer.

I was contemplating these lyrics and thought, Lord, *there are enough pain and difficulties in life that I'd sure like to avoid the needless pain!* I suspect that you feel the same way.

Two different proverbs (22:3 and 27:12, NLT) state, "A prudent person foresees danger and takes precautions. The simpleton goes blindly on and suffers the consequences." This clearly communicates that there are at least some problems we can avoid if we are prudent and exercise wisdom and foresight. For example, regularly changing the oil in the car is good for the engine and prolongs its life. If we drive 20,000 miles without changing the oil (when the manufacturer says it needs to be changed every 5,000 miles) and the engine burns up, we can't blame that problem on the devil, and we certainly shouldn't ask God why He allowed that to happen. If you're driving 17 miles an hour over the speed limit and get a ticket for speeding, don't tell people that "God allowed that for a purpose." No, *you* allowed it because you were driving too fast.

In Proverbs 1:20, Wisdom is seen crying out to give guidance. Those who refuse instruction suffer harm, while those who hearken to it receive great benefit.

For the turning away of the simple will slay them,
And the complacency of fools will destroy them;
But whoever listens to me will dwell safely,
And will be secure, without fear of evil.

Proverbs 1:32-33

Those who listen to wisdom will dwell safely, be secure, and live without fear of evil. Those are great benefits! Later in Proverbs, we see another benefit of hearkening to wisdom.

Hear, my son, and receive my sayings,
And the years of your life will be many.
I have taught you in the way of wisdom;
I have led you in right paths.
When you walk, your steps will not be hindered,
And when you run, you will not stumble.

Proverbs 4:10-12

There is no doubt in my mind, after reading these and many other scriptures, that there are some problems in life that we can prevent by walking in the wisdom of God. Other scriptures, though (such as Psalm 34:19 and John 16:33) lead me to believe that we can't avoid every problem that life has to offer.

Remember Reinhold Niebuhr's serenity prayer that states, "God grant me the serenity to accept the things I cannot change; courage to change the things I can; and wisdom to know the difference." Some things in life we can prevent. And sometimes, no matter what we do, there will still be problems to encounter. We need wisdom to know the difference, along with foresight to prevent the preventable problems and courage to deal with the problems we must face.

Everyone wants to avoid unnecessary trouble, but we need to keep in mind that Christianity is not about escapism. Saints throughout history, including Jesus, did not live their lives seeing how much trouble they could avoid; they lived their lives seeing how fully they could fulfill the plan of God, even when their obedience created certain problems for them.

Sometimes, the "problems" we face are other people. Paul made an interesting statement about dealing with people in Romans 12:18. He said, "If it is possible, as much as depends on you, live peaceably with all men." Think about that: "If it be possible..." and "...as much as it depends on you." This verse implies that sometimes "living peaceably" *won't* be possible and sometimes it depends on someone other than just you. In other words, Paul is encouraging us to do the best we can to get along with people, but in some cases it may not be possible because the decisions and actions of other people have a part to play.

You don't have authority over the free will of other people, nor can you control the decisions and actions of others, but you can take responsibility for yourself, for your attitudes, words, and actions. How you conduct yourself will influence what you experience in life.

He who would love life
And see good days,
Let him refrain his tongue from evil,
And his lips from speaking deceit.
Let him turn away from evil and do good;
Let him seek peace and pursue it.
For the eyes of the LORD are on the righteous,

And His ears are open to their prayers;
But the face of the Lord is against those who do evil."

1 Peter 3:10-12

Peter did not indicate that whether we love life and experience good days is entirely up to God. Of course, God is the Author of every good and perfect gift (James 1:17), but what we experience—according to Peter—is largely contingent on how we act. If you want to experience good days, do these things. It stands to reason that if you don't do those things, your days won't be all that good.

Our choices—how we carry ourselves and how we conduct ourselves—can affect the quality and quantity of our lives.

- "If you do this [listen to God], you will live many years, and your life will be satisfying" (Proverbs 3:2, NLT).
- "She [wisdom] offers you long life in her right hand, and riches and honor in her left" (Proverbs 3:16, NLT).
- "My child, listen to me and do as I say, and you will have a long, good life" (Proverbs 4:10, NLT).
- "Wisdom will multiply your days and add years to your life" (Proverbs 9:11, NLT).
- "Fear of the Lord lengthens one's life, but the years of the wicked are cut short" (Proverbs 10:27, NLT).
- "He who hates covetousness will prolong his days" (Proverbs 28:16).

If you walk in wisdom, will you avoid all problems? No. The Bible doesn't teach us that we can physically live forever or that we can avoid all problems if we just do everything right. But Scripture does teach, generally speaking, that we can improve the quantity and quality of our lives by following God. This chapter is titled "Can I Avoid At Least *Some* Problems?" and the answer is a resounding *yes*!

Wisdom at Work

Let's look at four examples from the New Testament where wisdom in operation averted certain problems.

> **After this Jesus went about in Galilee. He would not go about in Judea, because the Jews were seeking to kill him.**
>
> **John 7:1 (ESV)**

Notice the simple common sense in which Jesus walked. When people wanted to kill Jesus in Judea, he limited his exposure to that area. That's not to minimize Jesus' commitment to the will of God, but it wasn't time yet for Jesus to go to the cross. Therefore, He reduced unnecessary risk by being more guarded in His movements.

Shortly after his conversion, Paul (Saul) was targeted for assassination in Damascus. Notice the common sense steps that were followed as "Their plot became known to Saul. And they watched the gates day and night, to kill him. Then the disciples took him by night and let him down through the wall in a large basket" (Acts 9:24-25). Paul did not foolishly and presumptuously stay where he was, assuming that God would protect him. He got out of the city where people wanted to kill him.

During Paul's time in Ephesus, a massive demonstration took place in the great theater against Paul and his ministry.

Soon the whole city was filled with confusion. Everyone rushed to the amphitheater... Paul wanted to go in, too, but the believers wouldn't let him.

> **Some of the officials of the province, friends of Paul, also sent a message to him, begging him not to risk his life by entering the amphitheater.**
>
> **Acts 19:29-31 (NLT)**

Paul wanted to go in to that theater and defend the Gospel, but he eventually yielded to the good counsel of his friends. Proverbs 12:15 (NLT) says, "...the wise listen to others."

Later, when Paul was in prison in Jerusalem, people conspired to kill him. Paul did not know about the conspiracy, but his nephew did. "When Paul's sister's son heard of their ambush, he went and entered the barracks and told Paul. Then Paul called one of the centurions to him and said, 'Take this young man to the commander, for he has something to tell him'" (Acts 23:16-17).

In the three situations involving Paul, people did not merely respond spiritually. They took steps in the natural as well. Consider the following:

- In Damascus, Paul's fellow disciples took drastic action to help him get out of town.
- In Ephesus, Paul's friends restrained him from making a rash, unwise decision.
- In Jerusalem, Paul had his nephew report a threat against him to the authorities.

Paul is a unique case in that he was sent as a missionary to dangerous places and was called to write two-thirds of the New Testament as he spread the Gospel and evangelized much of the known world. However, we can relate the principles that Paul's experiences teach us and apply them to our own life. For example, if our vehicle breaks down, we might need help getting our car to the mechanic. If we need financial advice on an impending business decision, we should seek counsel from those who have wisdom in this area.

There are two mistakes that Christians often make in trying to deal with problems:

- Over-spiritualization: They try to deal with the problem only on a spiritual level without accessing and utilizing natural resources that are available.
- Isolation: They try to deal with the problem without anyone else's help or counsel.

Faith and prayer are always good, but natural help is also important. Proverbs 21:31 says, "The horse is prepared for the day of battle, but deliverance is of the LORD." God is not just the God of the supernatural; He made natural things for us to benefit from, use, and enjoy.

Likewise, other people can help us find success in life. Woodrow Wilson said, "I not only use all the brains that I have, but all I can borrow." Henry J. Kaiser remarked, "I make progress by having people around me who are smarter than I am—and listening to them. And I assume that everyone is smarter about something than I am." We would be wise to find people to help us in our time of need—and to seek people who specialize in the area that we need help in.

Strategic relationships can be very beneficial. I'm not talking about having a utilitarian approach to friendship. I'm not even talking about turning to friends necessarily. Often, in addition to seeking and trusting God, we can seek out professionals who are better equipped to help us in the particular situation we are facing. Money problems? Talk to a banker or financial advisor. Health issues? Talk to a doctor or nutritionist. If you think you know everything and that you don't have to rely on anyone else to help you in life, you're probably going to have a much harder time than if you benefitted from the skills and knowledge of others. Paul let other people help him, and we should as well.

Can you control everything in life? Certainly not, and you will create a high level of angst for yourself if you try. But can you make wise decisions and take prudent actions that will help create a better life for you? Absolutely.

When it comes to choices, I love what God said to the children of Israel through Moses.

> **I call heaven and earth as witnesses today against you, that I have set before you life and death, blessing and cursing; therefore choose life, that both you and your descendants may live; that you may love the LORD your God, that you may obey His voice, and that you may cling to Him, for He is your life and the length of your days; and that you may dwell in the land which the LORD swore to your fathers, to Abraham, Isaac, and Jacob, to give them.**
>
> **Deuteronomy 30:19-20**

Let's choose life and blessing by loving, obeying, and clinging to our wonderful God in every dimension of our lives.

Concluding Thought: We can't control everything in the universe, but we have a significant amount of influence on many things we experience in life. God makes it clear in His Word that we have choices to make, and that our choices have consequences.

Questions for Reflection and Discussion

1. Have you ever tried so hard to avoid problems that you failed to enjoy life? Is that going on in your life now? If so, what can you do about it?

2. In this chapter, we talked about the needless pain that people sometimes experience. Have you ever experienced needless pain in your life? Did you recognize that it was unnecessary and take steps to change whatever was causing you pain?
3. We read the proverb that says a prudent person foresees danger and takes precautions. Can you think of times in the past where you've followed that adage, and how it's benefitted you? Are there any potential problems that you can address on a proactive, preventative basis now?
4. Have you ever blamed God or the devil for something that was really just the result of a bad decision on your part? How and when did you get honest with yourself? How does it make you feel when you hear other people blaming God or the devil for their own mistakes?
5. In this chapter, we read that we don't have authority over the free will of other people, nor can we control the decisions and actions of others. Have you come to terms with this truth? Do you find yourself trying to control outcomes in other people's lives? What have you done about this tendency in the past, and what can you do about it in the present?
6. How successful are you at balancing the spiritual and natural aspects of life? Do you feel that you appropriately consider both sides when you're trying to solve problems? How are you at seeking out wisdom and assistance from others?

Chapter Nine

Storm Chasers

By yourself you're unprotected. With a friend you can face the worst. Can you round up a third? A three-stranded rope isn't easily snapped.
- Ecclesiastes 4:12 (MSG)

Key Thought: Storm chasers are those rare individuals who run *toward* the storm—for the sake of others—when everyone else is taking cover.

Having lived in Oklahoma for more than three decades, Lisa and I have been through many active tornado seasons. In addition to the meteorologists with their high tech radar systems, some of the people who receive significant attention during tornado season are the storm chasers. These are individuals who are outside looking for storms when others are looking out for themselves. While a few storm chasers may be self-appointed, reckless thrill seekers, others are assisting the weathermen to know what to report, and hopefully, helping to protect others and save lives.

In life, there are some people we might also call "storm chasers." These are individuals who come into our lives when we're in the midst of the storm. Instead of pursuing their own leisure and comfort, they come to encourage, to offer emotional and spiritual support, and to help us walk through our storm.

Maybe you've been through a turbulent season in your life only to find that those you thought were your friends were nowhere to be found. Walter Winchell said, "A real friend is someone who walks in when the rest of the world walks out." Perhaps you've been blessed to have good, loving people offer support to you during a time of upheaval in your life, and maybe you've had the privilege of being a storm chaser to someone else. Maybe you've been able to bring stability, support, and strength to someone during a difficult phase of his or her journey.

Jesus spoke very highly of storm chasers. Let's look at one such passage in Matthew chapter 25.

> **Then the King will say to those on His right hand, "Come, you blessed of My Father, inherit the kingdom prepared for you from the foundation of the world: for I was hungry and you gave Me food; I was thirsty and you gave Me drink; I was a stranger and you took Me in; I was naked and you clothed Me; I was sick and you visited Me; I was in prison and you came to Me."**
>
> **Then the righteous will answer Him, saying, "Lord, when did we see You hungry and feed You, or thirsty and give You drink? When did we see You a stranger and take You in, or naked and clothe You? Or when did we see You sick, or in prison, and come to You?" And the King will answer and say to them, "Assuredly, I say to you, inasmuch as you did it to one of the least of these My brethren, you did it to Me."**
>
> **Matthew 25:34-40**

Notice what these righteous individuals did. While others avoided or ignored those in need, these godly storm chasers stepped into their troubled world and offered support. Similarly, Hebrews 13:3 says, "Remember those in prison, as if you were there yourself. Remember also those being mistreated, as if you felt their pain in your own bodies" (NLT).

The Apostle Paul was not only a man who had comforted many in their distress, but he was also a man who had been comforted when he himself was struggling. He referred to God as "our merciful Father and the source of all comfort," and said that "He comforts us in all our troubles so that we can comfort others. When they are troubled, we will be able to give them the same comfort God has given us" (2 Corinthians 1:3-4, NLT).

On a related note, D.L. Moody said, "It seems to me the basest ingratitude if we do not reach out the hand to others who are down in the same pit from which we were delivered." This principle so clearly reflects what Jesus taught: "Freely you have received, freely give" (Matthew 10:8). I don't for a minute believe that God does bad things to us so that we can help others to whom He's doing bad things. But life is simply full of bad things and when we've been through some of them, we have a greater capacity to show understanding and compassion (at least, we should) and to help others who are going through the same kinds of things.

Recovery groups have long understood that part of restoration to wholeness involves not just receiving help, but also then endeavoring to help others as well. What's the bottom line? When God has helped you, don't let it stop with you. Extend that same help toward others.

Again, the Apostle Paul himself had received comfort and encouragement from others. Let's look at three of these instances.

Remember when Paul went through the terrible storm in Acts 27? After that, the ship was destroyed and he swam to shore. It was cold and wet, and a snake bit him. From a circumstantial standpoint, it was a very, very difficult season in his life. When Paul finally was making his way toward Rome as a prisoner, we read, "...and so we came to Rome. The believers in Rome heard about us, and came as far as the towns of Market of Appius and Three Inns to meet us. When Paul saw them, he thanked God and was greatly encouraged" (Acts 28:14-15, GNB).

I wonder how tired Paul might have been at that point. What was it about this "cheering section" that brought great encouragement to Paul? There was something about the presence of these believers showing love and concern for Paul that really ministered to him. Think about others who might be weary from their journey and their storms and see if you might become an encourager to them.

Paul described another difficult time in his life and gave great testimony as to how God helped him through his friend and associate Titus.

> **When we came to Macedonia, our bodies had no rest, but we were troubled on every side. Outside were conflicts, inside were fears. Nevertheless God, who comforts the downcast, comforted us by the coming of Titus....**
>
> **2 Corinthians 7:5-6**

Paul mentions that there was trouble all around him—external conflicts and internal fears. God's solution to this problem situation was to comfort Paul by sending Titus to him. Perhaps a friend has been sent to you just when you needed comfort the most. Perhaps now you can be sent to comfort someone else who is currently troubled.

A third time that Paul found encouragement is related in his final epistle—Second Timothy. Paul had a very special friend named Onesiphorus. When Paul was in prison, a lot of his friends decided to not associate with him anymore. However, Onesiphorus was one of those rare individuals who walked into Paul's life when everyone else was walking out.

Consider how much Paul treasured and valued the love that was extended to him by his dear, faithful friend.

> **May the Lord show special kindness to Onesiphorus and all his family because he often visited and encouraged me. He was never ashamed of me because I was in chains. When he came to Rome, he searched everywhere until he found me. May the Lord show him special kindness on the day of Christ's return. And you know very well how helpful he was in Ephesus.**
>
> **2 Timothy 1:16-18 (NLT)**

Maybe you're reading about all these wonderful people who came into Paul's life—the storm chasers who came to him in troubled times—and you're thinking, *God, I need a cheering section like Paul had. I need a Titus to comfort me. I need an Onesiphorus to encourage and be helpful to me.* If God has given someone like that to you now or in the past, consider yourself blessed. And by all means, make sure that you take on the role of comforter and encourager toward others.

The Worst Storm Chasers Ever

In ancient times, physicians who took the Hippocratic Oath pledged to "do no harm." That's a good commitment for physicians, and it's also a good commitment for all who minister to people struggling and fighting their way through the storms of life.

In the Book of Job, the central figure of this book had experienced massive loss in his life. His ten children had died, his financial empire had collapsed, many of his employees had died, and his health failed. In the midst of this, his wife's only recorded suggestion was to tell him to "curse God and die" (Job 2:9).

In the midst of Job's intense and agonizing suffering, he made the following statement:

> **"My relatives stay far away,**
> **and my friends have turned against me.**
> **My family is gone,**
> **and my close friends have forgotten me.**
> **My breath is repulsive to my wife.**
> **I am rejected by my own family.**
> **Even young children despise me.**
> **When I stand to speak, they turn their backs on me.**
> **My close friends detest me.**
> **Those I loved have turned against me."**
>
> **Job 19:13-14, 17-19 (NLT)**

What isolation Job was experiencing! How tragic that on top of all of the other tragedies in his life, he also felt such intense loneliness and isolation. Suffering immensely on his own, Job needed a friend to comfort him. Instead of many people surrounding Job to help him get back up, Job was surrounded by three men who seemed to do nothing but kick Job while he was down and pour salt in his wounds. I want to study these men and learn from their mistakes, and discover what storm chasers ought *not* to do.

At first, those who went to Job seemed to have good intentions, and they appeared to start out well in providing support and comfort to him.

> **Now when Job's three friends heard of all this adversity that had come upon him, each one came from his own place—Eliphaz the Temanite, Bildad the Shuhite, and Zophar the Naamathite. For they had made an appointment together to come and mourn with him, and to comfort him. And when they raised their eyes from afar, and did not recognize him, they lifted their voices and**

wept; and each one tore his robe and sprinkled dust on his head toward heaven. So they sat down with him on the ground seven days and seven nights, and no one spoke a word to him, for they saw that his grief was very great.

Job 2:11-13

In the presence of overwhelming grief, there are times when "the ministry of presence" is the most comforting thing. Giving comfort is not found in offering platitudes or clichés, but in just being with the person who is in pain. In this regard, Job's three friends did a good job in the first part of their time as storm chasers.

Afterward, Job began to erupt in complaints, expressing not only his deep pain, but also his profound misperceptions of God. Job saw God as sadistic, cruel, unjust, adversarial, and aloof. He perceived God as taking great delight in torturing and tormenting him. When God confronted Job and gave Job more insight into His true nature, Job replied, "I'm speechless, in awe—words fail me. I should never have opened my mouth! I've talked too much, way too much. I'm ready to shut up and listen" (Job 40:3-4, MSG). Job also said, "I was talking about things I knew nothing about, things far too wonderful for me...I take back everything I said, and I sit in dust and ashes to show my repentance" (Job 42:3, 6, NLT).[11]

When Job was making some of his erroneous statements, his three so-called friends, the storm chasers, attacked him with great harshness. They said that God was punishing him because of his wickedness, and that God wasn't even punishing him as much as he deserved. Late in the book, Job gets angry: "...against his three friends his wrath was aroused, because they had found no answer, and yet had condemned Job" (32:3). God Himself

[11] While Job said several wrong things about God, there are also many glimmers of glorious light that came from his mouth (e.g., Job 19:25-27). Some of his statements very accurately portray an awareness of his deficiencies and his hunger for greater knowledge of God (e.g., Job 9:2, 11, 32-33; 23:3, 8-10, 12).

spoke to the three toxic storm chasers and said, "...you have not spoken of Me what is right..." (Job 42:7).

The Bible says that we are supposed to speak the truth to one another in love (Ephesians 4:15). The condemning, accusatory statements that Job's three "friends" made to him were neither true nor loving. Instead of helping Job, they made the whole situation harder for him. Job lashed out at his friends, reacting harshly to their remarks with some caustic words of his own.

> **As for you, you smear me with lies. As physicians, you are worthless quacks. If only you could be silent! That's the wisest thing you could do.**
>
> **Job 13:4-5 (NLT)**

> **I have heard many such things; Miserable comforters are you all!**
>
> **Job 16:2**

> **How long will you torture me? How long will you try to crush me with your words? You have already insulted me ten times. You should be ashamed of treating me so badly.**
>
> **Job 19:2-3 (NLT)**

Job really didn't appreciate the "comfort" he received from his storm-chasing friends. As a matter of fact, part of God's restoration plan for Job included having Job pray for these men who had added so much insult to Job's injuries. Job 42:10 says, "When Job prayed for his friends, the LORD restored his fortunes. In fact, the LORD gave him twice as much as before" (NLT).

If you're going to be a storm chaser, make sure that you're a blessing, help, and encouragement to those to whom you minister. Lift people; don't put them down! Follow Paul's advice and "Rejoice with those who rejoice, and weep with those who weep" (Romans 12:15).

God intended that we find support, encouragement, and help in our relationships with other believers. Earlier in this chapter, we looked at three times Paul was encouraged and helped by others, but let's look at one more.

> **They stoned Paul and dragged him out of the town, thinking he was dead. But the disciples formed a circle around him, and he got back up and went back to town.**
>
> **Acts 14:19-20 (ISV)**

I love that image! When Paul had been pummeled by rocks and left for dead, his fellow believers "formed a circle around him." I feel sure they were praying for Paul, and the results seem to be nothing short of miraculous! Other translations of verse 20 say "the believers gathered around him" (NLT) and "the disciples surrounded him" (HCSB).

In similar fashion, when Peter and John were released from prison, "they went to their own company" (Acts 4:23, KJV). Other translations say that Peter and John

- "went to their own companions" (NKJV).
- "went to their friends" (ESV).
- "went to their own people" (HCSB).
- "went to their own group" (NCV).

I pray that you are a part of a good church and that you have strong relationships with other believers. We need friends in good times, but if you ever face a significant crisis, you will need companions and friends—people who can form a circle around you, gather around you with kindness, and surround you with support. There will also be times when you need to be part of a circle of support for others.

Tips for Storm Chasers

In order to be the kind of friend that people turn to in crises, we need to be sure not to follow the example of Job's three friends. Here are some tips on how we can be the kind of storm chaser others want and need in their life when the storm hits.

- Make sure you really love people. This won't work well without love and compassion.
- Be quick to listen, slow to speak.
- Offer the ministry of presence.
- Offer practical help.
- Gently and kindly infuse faith and hope into every situation. Maintain and project an attitude of positive expectancy toward God in the situation.
- Don't be afraid to say "I don't know" to certain questions.
- Don't feel like you need to offer religious platitudes or philosophical clichés.
- Don't say, "I know just how you feel..." and try to force your testimony on the other person.
- Don't feel like you have to do everything yourself. Enlist the help of others.

Encourage the development of a support network. Make referrals to professionals if needed, and to those with specific skills and gifts. Gary Collins wrote, "Even the Good Samaritan got the injured man to the inn, helped him on the road to recovery, and then left. We are not called to be rescuers whose personal self-esteem depends on our unhealthy needs to have others be dependent on us."[12]

- Be careful that you don't get overwhelmed with the burdens of others. Romans 12:8 says, "...if you work with the disadvantaged, don't let yourself get irritated with them or depressed by them" (MSG).
- Don't feel the pressure to "fix" people or solve all of their problems. You have limitations in the situation. You can help and encourage people, but God has His responsibilities and the person has responsibilities as well. Don't take on responsibilities that are not yours, and realize that often the recovery process takes time.
- Follow up with people. Don't just help during the immediate crisis. Be sensitive to the fact that many people benefit from on-going support and encouragement.

If we are careful to be this kind of friend in other people's time of need, we are more likely to receive this same kind of friendship from other storm chasers when we are in trouble (Proverbs 18:24).

Having said all of this about friendships and relationships, we should remember that our ultimate trust must be in God. People can let us down, which is why Psalm 118:8-9 says, "It is better to trust in the LORD than to put confidence in man. It is better to trust in the LORD than to put confidence in princes." We studied several examples from Paul's life when he received help and encouragement from others, but he also faced a critical point in his life where no friends came through for him.

---

[12] Gary R. Collins, *How to be a People Helper: The Techniques of Helping People.* (Carol Stream, Illinois: Tyndale House Publishers, 1995).

At my first defense no one stood with me, but all forsook me. May it not be charged against them. But the Lord stood with me and strengthened me, so that the message might be preached fully through me, and that all the Gentiles might hear. Also I was delivered out of the mouth of the lion. And the Lord will deliver me from every evil work and preserve me for His heavenly kingdom. To Him be glory forever and ever. Amen!

2 Timothy 4:16-18

During this particular storm, no one except the Lord stood with Paul. Paul's friends and companions forsook him, but the Lord strengthened him so that Paul was able to continue fulfilling God's plan for his life.

It is wonderful when God works through His people to bring comfort and aid, but we must always keep our eyes on God whether others do the right thing or not.

Concluding Thought: Storm chasers are those rare individuals who run *toward* the storm—for the sake of others—when everyone else is taking cover.

Questions for Reflection and Discussion

1. Can you think of anyone who has been a storm chaser in your life? Has someone been a true friend who walked into your life when it seemed like everyone else was walking out? What role did that person play in your life, and in what ways did he or she help you through your storm?
2. Are there any specific issues or storms that you've survived that have enabled you to be compassionate and understanding toward those facing similar situations? How have you been able to use your own experiences to help others?
3. Even though we consider the Apostle Paul a spiritual giant, there were times when he struggled. During the hard times, Paul truly benefitted from "the storm chasers" in his life—and he greatly appreciated them too. Do you think it was difficult for Paul to acknowledge his own needs and to receive help from others? Why or why not? Has pride kept you from acknowledging the storms in your life or from receiving help from other people? How open are you to receiving help from others?
4. Has one of "Job's comforters" ever come to you and made your storm passage more difficult? Have you ever inadvertently made someone else's journey more difficult because of a lack of understanding or sensitivity on your part?
5. Review the tips for storm chasers. Were you already aware of most of these points? Have you successfully implemented some of these tips in the past as you sought to help people? Were any of these tips new to you? If so, do you see how they could have been helpful to you in the past?

6. Read James 5:13-20 and consider the significance of good relationships with believers. How important is the local church in your life when it comes to having support when you face storms, and offering support when others are going through difficult times?

Chapter Ten

Suffering and the Will of God

They gave our Master a crown of thorns. Why do we hope for a crown of roses?

- Martin Luther

Key Thought: The Bible addresses different types of suffering, and different principles apply accordingly. Peter said, "...let those who suffer according to the will of God commit their souls to Him in doing good, as to a faithful Creator" (1 Peter 4:19). If there is a suffering that is according to the will of God, it stands to reason that there is a suffering that is not according to the will of God. May God give us the wisdom to know the difference, and the grace to persevere through life's necessary challenges.

There are more opinions and deep feelings about the issue of suffering than perhaps any other subject. When we have suffered pain or loss, we want to make sense of it and find some kind of meaning. Some people ascribe the suffering to God, while others may attribute negative events to demonic powers or bad people. Others accredit problems and pain to randomness and chance.

The Problem with Blaming God

In trying to provide some type of spiritual context for suffering, some have attributed tragedies to a mysterious, incomprehensible God. I remember reading the story of a family whose young son had just died. Some well-meaning Christian, probably assuming he was being helpful in some way, told the boy's unsaved father, "God took your boy so you'd get saved." The man responded, "If God did that, to hell with him," and stormed out of the room.[13] Obviously, that father wanted nothing to do with a God who would cause that kind of suffering in order to bring him to salvation.

So if suffering doesn't come from God, where does it come from? I find much wisdom in what author Richard Exley shared:

> In my counseling with those who question why humans must suffer, sometimes I simplistically explain that we inhabit a planet which is in rebellion, that we are part of a race living outside God's will, and that one consequence of that rebellion is sickness and death. God doesn't send this plague upon people, nor does He will it. It is simply a natural consequence of humanity's fallen state. Although as believers, we are a new creation in Christ (2 Corinthians 5:17), we remain a part of this human family—a family that is tainted by sin and death. As a consequence, we too suffer the inevitable repercussions of that fallen state, even though we may be personally committed to the doing of God's will and the coming of His kingdom. In truth, the cause of sickness and death is not God, but the hated enemy, sin. Not our personal sin necessarily, not a specific sin—for life and death cannot be reduced to a mathematical equation—but the fact of sin.[14]

[13] Kenneth E. Hagin, *Health Food Devotions* (Tulsa, OK: Faith Library Publications, 2007), 194.
[14] Richard Exley, *When You Lose Someone You Love* (Colorado Springs, CO: David C. Cook, 2009).

Here are some very important truths for us—members of the human family–to consider regarding suffering:

- Before sin entered the world, God had looked at His entire creation and said that it was "very good" (Genesis 1:31). There was no sickness, no pain, no lack, no sorrow, no hatred, and no violence.
- When Satan and evil have been vanquished from the world—when the new heaven and new earth appear—Revelation 21:4 says, "God will wipe away every tear from their eyes; there shall be no more death, nor sorrow, nor crying. There shall be no more pain, for the former things have passed away."
- Jesus consistently alleviated human suffering. Throughout His earthly ministry, Jesus went about "doing good and healing all who were oppressed by the devil, for God was with Him" (Acts 10:38). Matthew 9:35 says, "Jesus went about all the cities and villages, teaching in their synagogues, preaching the gospel of the kingdom, and healing every sickness and every disease among the people."
- Jesus said, "The thief does not come except to steal, and to kill, and to destroy. I have come that they may have life, and that they may have it more abundantly" (John 10:10).
- Jesus also taught his disciples to pray, "Your kingdom come. Your will be done on earth as it is in heaven" (Matthew 6:10; Luke 11:2).
- James 1:17 says, "Every good gift and every perfect gift is from above, and comes down from the Father of lights, with whom there is no variation or shadow of turning." First John 1:5 declares, "God is light and in Him is no darkness at all."

These scriptures and principles express the heart of God. Had sin never entered the world, suffering wouldn't have entered it either. But we don't live in an ideal world; we live in a fallen world, and we see the effects of sin all around us. Creation itself is reeling from the aftermath and weight of sin.

> **...the creation itself will also be set free from the bondage of corruption into the glorious freedom of God's children. For we know that the whole creation has been groaning together with labor pains until now. And not only that, but we ourselves who have the Spirit as the firstfruits—we also groan within ourselves, eagerly waiting for adoption, the redemption of our bodies.**
>
> **Romans 8:21-23 (HCSB)**

Creation awaits full redemption, as do we. Verse 23 says that we "eagerly wait for adoption, the redemption of our bodies." Our bodies still endure human limitations, and Paul even said that, "...our outward man is perishing" (2 Corinthians 4:16). When people experience challenges and vulnerabilities, they often want to know *why*.

Beyond the influence of "cosmic corruption," we still look for insights into the particular sources of pain and sadness. Specifically, people sometimes suffer because of deliberate, malevolent actions of evil people. In other cases, suffering can occur because of an accident or mishap, even though no harmful intentions were involved. Jesus addressed both scenarios.

> **About this time Jesus was informed that Pilate had murdered some people from Galilee as they were offering sacrifices at the Temple. "Do you think those Galileans were worse sinners than all the other people from Galilee?" Jesus asked. "Is that why they suffered? Not at all! And you will perish, too, unless you repent of your sins and turn to God. And what about the eighteen**

people who died when the tower in Siloam fell on them? Were they the worst sinners in Jerusalem? No, and I tell you again that unless you repent, you will perish, too."

Luke 13:1-5 (NLT)

While Jesus provides no comprehensive explanation as to why bad things happen, He does make it clear that these people did not experience their demise because of some specific sin they had committed. Instead, Jesus points to the universality of death and indicates the widespread need for all of mankind to repent—to turn from sin and put their faith in God. Instead of addressing the specifics of these two situations, Jesus highlights the need of all people to escape the death that sin brings and to embrace the salvation that God offers. In doing this, Jesus emphasizes the big picture.

Jesus Our Substitute

There are some ways in which Jesus suffered in our place, as our substitute. He did this so that we would not have to suffer in the same way. For example, Jesus bore the punishment for our sin so that we would not have to. Second Corinthians 5:21 says, "[God] made Him who knew no sin to be sin for us, that we might become the righteousness of God in Him." Jesus took our place so that we could be completely liberated from guilt, shame, and condemnation. He bore the wrath of God so that we could experience the peace of God. He experienced alienation from God (Matthew 27:46) so that we could experience union with God. Isaiah 53:5 says, "He was wounded for our transgressions, He was bruised for our iniquities; The chastisement for our peace was upon Him, and by His stripes we are healed."

On this subject of Jesus being our substitute, I like what J.C. Ryle has to say:

> The Lord Jesus Christ, in great love and compassion, has made a full and complete satisfaction for sin, by suffering death in our place upon the cross. There He offered Himself as a sacrifice for us, and allowed the wrath of God, which we deserved, to fall on His own head. For our sins, as our Substitute, He gave Himself, suffered, and died—the just for the unjust, the innocent for the guilty—that He might deliver us from the curse of a broken law, and provide a complete pardon for all who are willing to receive it.[15]

Because Jesus was our substitute, we don't have to earn God's favor or work for salvation. These are freely given to believers because of the price that Jesus paid on our behalf.

Jesus Our Example

While Jesus suffered as our substitute, there are other ways in which Jesus suffered as our example. He demonstrated what it means to be a godly person in an ungodly world. He modeled grace under fire. He showed what it is to exhibit love to the unloving and to display kindness to the cruel. He personified unconditional trust, unwavering obedience, and an unflinching commitment to do the will of God whatever the cost. We see the example Jesus set for us in many passages in Peter's first epistle.

> **For this is commendable, if because of conscience toward God one endures grief, suffering wrongfully. For what credit is it if, when you are beaten for your faults, you take it patiently? But when you do good and suffer, if you take it patiently, this is commendable before God. For to this you were called, because Christ also suffered for us, leaving us an example, that**

[15]J.C. Ryle, "Christ Our Great Substitute," *J.C. Ryle Quotes.com* http://jcrylequotes.com/2012/03/01/christ-our-great-substitute/ (accessed April 22, 2013).

you should follow His steps: "Who committed no sin, nor was deceit found in His mouth"; who, when He was reviled, did not revile in return; when He suffered, He did not threaten, but committed Himself to Him who judges righteously.

1 Peter 2:19-23

But even if you should suffer for righteousness' sake, you are blessed. "And do not be afraid of their threats, nor be troubled." But sanctify the Lord God in your hearts, and always be ready to give a defense to everyone who asks you a reason for the hope that is in you, with meekness and fear; having a good conscience, that when they defame you as evildoers, those who revile your good conduct in Christ may be ashamed. For it is better, if it is the will of God, to suffer for doing good than for doing evil.

1 Peter 3:14-17

Therefore, since Christ suffered for us in the flesh, arm yourselves also with the same mind, for he who has suffered in the flesh has ceased from sin, that he no longer should live the rest of his time in the flesh for the lusts of men, but for the will of God. For we have spent enough of our past lifetime in doing the will of the Gentiles—when we walked in lewdness, lusts, drunkenness, revelries, drinking parties, and abominable idolatries. In regard to these, they think it strange that you do not run with them in the same flood of dissipation, speaking evil of you. They will give an account to Him who is ready to judge the living and the dead.

1 Peter 4:1-5

Beloved, do not think it strange concerning the fiery trial which is to try you, as though some strange thing happened to you; but rejoice to the extent that you partake of Christ's sufferings, that

> **when His glory is revealed, you may also be glad with exceeding joy. If you are reproached for the name of Christ, blessed are you, for the Spirit of glory and of God rests upon you. On their part He is blasphemed, but on your part He is glorified. But let none of you suffer as a murderer, a thief, an evildoer, or as a busybody in other people's matters. Yet if anyone suffers as a Christian, let him not be ashamed, but let him glorify God in this matter. Therefore let those who suffer according to the will of God commit their souls to Him in doing good, as to a faithful Creator.**
>
> **1 Peter 4:12-16, 19**

> **Be sober, be vigilant; because your adversary the devil walks about like a roaring lion, seeking whom he may devour. Resist him, steadfast in the faith, knowing that the same sufferings are experienced by your brotherhood in the world. But may the God of all grace, who called us to His eternal glory by Christ Jesus, after you have suffered a while, perfect, establish, strengthen, and settle you.**
>
> **1 Peter 5:8-10**

This kind of suffering listed in First Peter is not to be avoided or "prayed away." Jesus suffered in this way as our example. This kind of persecution will happen as believers follow God in a fallen world.

Suffering in the Life of Paul

Jesus wasn't the only one to suffer for following God's plan. Immediately after Paul's conversion on the road to Damascus, Jesus spoke to a disciple named Ananias and directed him to go and pray for Paul.

> **But the Lord said to him, "Go, for he is a chosen vessel of Mine to bear My name before Gentiles, kings, and the children of Israel. For I will show him how many things he must suffer for My name's sake."**
>
> **Acts 9:15-16**

According to this passage, Paul suffered simply for bearing the name of Christ—for being an influential Christian. After many years of ministry, Paul described his experiences to his young protégé, Timothy.

> **But you have carefully followed my doctrine, manner of life, purpose, faith, longsuffering, love, perseverance, persecutions, afflictions, which happened to me at Antioch, at Iconium, at Lystra—what persecutions I endured. And out of them all the Lord delivered me. Yes, and all who desire to live godly in Christ Jesus will suffer persecution.**
>
> **2 Timothy 3:10-12**

Paul listed a myriad of painful experiences he underwent in his quest to obey God and fully proclaim the Gospel (see 2 Corinthians 11:22-29). In light of the assaults and harassments inspired by this "messenger of Satan," Jesus admonished Paul, "My grace is sufficient for you, for My strength is made perfect in weakness" (2 Corinthians 12:9). Paul had learned the vital lesson "that we should not trust in ourselves but in God who raises the dead" (2 Corinthians 1:9).

Could Paul have avoided some of these persecutions? Absolutely. All he needed to do was to compromise his faith, back off from his message, relinquish his assignment, and blend in with the world. He would still have faced the normal, day-to-day challenges that all humans face, but he would have no longer been the target for intense ridicule, rabid hostility, and vicious spiritual attacks.

To Paul, obedience to the will of God was far more important than personal comfort, and his perspective—how he saw things—contributed greatly to his ability to endure.

> **Therefore we do not lose heart. Even though our outward man is perishing, yet the inward man is being renewed day by day. For our light affliction, which is but for a moment, is working for us a far more exceeding and eternal weight of glory, while we do not look at the things which are seen, but at the things which are not seen. For the things which are seen are temporary, but the things which are not seen are eternal.**
>
> **2 Corinthians 4:16-18**

Paul called what he was experiencing a light and momentary affliction; he placed more value and focus on the eternal reward that awaited him. Paul followed in the footsteps of Moses, who chose "to suffer affliction with the people of God, than to enjoy the pleasures of sin for a season" (Hebrews 11:25, KJV).

The book of Hebrews also describes faith-filled believers who stood powerfully in the face of great adversity.

> **...you remained faithful even though it meant terrible suffering. Sometimes you were exposed to public ridicule and were beaten, and sometimes you helped others who were suffering the same things. You suffered along with those who were thrown into jail, and when all you owned was taken from you, you accepted it with joy. You knew there were better things waiting for you that will last forever.**
>
> **Hebrews 10:32-34 (NLT)**

This kind of suffering—public ridicule, beatings, jail time—does not sound like fun! But these believers who suffered for simply professing and preaching the Gospel, accepted it with joy because, like Paul, they kept their focus on the eternal.

Jesus told His disciples that everyone would hate them for His name's sake (Matthew 10:22). He also said, "'A servant is not greater than his master.' If they persecuted Me, they will also persecute you" (John 15:20). When Stephen, the first martyr of the Church was put to death, Jesus stood up to honor him and welcome him home (Acts 7:55-56). Jesus told the Church at Smyrna, "Do not fear any of those things which you are about to suffer. Indeed, the devil is about to throw some of you into prison, that you may be tested, and you will have tribulation ten days. Be faithful until death, and I will give you the crown of life" (Revelation 2:10). To the Church of Pergamos, Jesus honored "Antipas... My faithful martyr, who was killed among you" (Revelation 2:13). Jesus makes it clear that Christians will suffer persecution for their faith.

G.K. Chesterton said, "Jesus promised his disciples three things—that they would be completely fearless, absurdly happy, and in constant trouble." The truth of his statement is seen in Acts 5:40-42 (NCV), where the apostles are punished by the religious leaders for their proclamation of the gospel. "They called the apostles in, beat them, and told them not to speak in the name of Jesus again. Then they let them go free. The apostles left the meeting full of joy because they were given the honor of suffering disgrace for Jesus. Every day in the Temple and in people's homes they continued teaching the people and telling the Good News—that Jesus is the Christ." Contrary to what you might have heard and what many claim, "suffering for Jesus" isn't about being sick or broke; it's about being persecuted by the world for being a follower of Christ. However, just like the Apostles in Acts chapter 5, we can be full of joy when we are persecuted for doing what's right or when we suffer for being godly in an ungodly world.

It's Okay Not to Know Everything

I don't pretend to know and understand everything there is in life. Thank God for what He has revealed to us in His Word, but we are certainly not omniscient, or all-knowing. First Corinthians 13:12 says, "Now we see things imperfectly, like puzzling reflections in a mirror, but then we will see everything with perfect clarity. All that I know now is partial and incomplete, but then I will know everything completely, just as God now knows me completely" (NLT). Because I only know in part, I don't understand why some people get healed and some don't, or why some Christians live a long life while others go to Heaven due to accidents or tragedies.

Two stark verses (Acts 12:1-2) describe the brutal death of James, the brother of John: "Now about that time Herod the king stretched out his hand to harass some from the church. Then he killed James the brother of John with the sword." There is nothing flowery about that remark; it's just a plain statement of fact. Most Christians never give much thought to those two verses, but we celebrate the next seventeen verses (Acts 12:3-19), which gloriously describe the deliverance of Peter from Herod in vivid detail.

Did you ever stop to ask yourself, *Why did Peter get delivered right after James was put to death? Why did one person get a miracle and the other did not?* Of course, theories can be made about the plan of God for Peter's life and so forth, but regardless of how theologically correct those ideas might be, I doubt they would have done much to soothe the agony that Zebedee and Salome, James' parents, would have been feeling when their son was murdered.

If James' parents were still alive at the time of his death, I can only hope that the Church (who rightly celebrated Peter's deliverance) was as effective at "weeping with those who weep" as they were in "rejoicing with those who rejoice" (Romans 12:15). I certainly hope that no one came up to them and suggested that James must have missed God, lacked faith, or had sin in his life.

The Bible simply does not explain why Paul left Trophimus sick in Miletus (2 Timothy 4:20), why John the Baptist died in prison after hearing about the miracles of deliverance Jesus performed for others, or why Peter was miraculously rescued from prison but James was not. As much as people sometimes don't like to hear it, there are still "secret things" that belong to the Lord our God (Deuteronomy 29:29). During the times when we have more questions than answers, perhaps we can find comfort in the words of Thomas Moore who said, "Earth has no sorrow that heaven cannot heal." Bad things happen to good people, and we don't always know why. But we know that God can soothe our pain and mend our broken hearts, providing us a peace that surpasses our understanding (Philippians 4:7)—a peace that only He can give.

Scripture clearly shows us instances where the faith of certain individuals was an integral part of prayers being answered and desires being granted in the here-and-now:

- The woman with the issue of blood (Mark 5:34)
- The centurion (Matthew 8:13)
- The lame man in Lystra (Acts 14:9-10)

But there are also examples in Scripture where faith seems to be more of a *transcendent* faith, which is to say, an over-arching faith in God Himself that remained strong in spite of seemingly unanswered prayers. Habakkuk, the prophet of the Old Testament, described an unconditional faith in God, a faith that transcended specific results (or lack of results) and still looked confidently and expectantly toward the future.

Though the fig tree may not blossom,
nor fruit be on the vines;
Though the labor of the olive may fail,
and the fields yield no food;
Though the flock may be cut off from the fold,
and there be no herd in the stalls—
Yet I will rejoice in the LORD,
I will joy in the God of my salvation.
The LORD God is my strength;
He will make my feet like deer's feet,
and He will make me walk on my high hills.

Habakkuk 3:17-19

May I propose a paraphrase of the prophet's words? When everything that could possibly go wrong goes wrong, and when anything that could possibly go right doesn't go right—I'm still going to keep my faith in God. Trusting God should not be restricted to procuring certain results nor is it to be deterred by a lack of results. Our faith should transcend any and all circumstances and rest only in Him. Then, each of us can say, "I will continue to rejoice in Him, and be confident that He will make me victorious in the end."

When faced with a situation that we don't understand, it is important that we follow the wise advice of Scripture: "Trust in the LORD with all your heart, and lean not on your own understanding; In all your ways acknowledge Him, and He shall direct your paths" (Proverbs 3:5-6).

Our Attitude Matters

It's often been said that trials and adversity will make us bitter or better. We certainly see this to be true in the case of Joseph. If ever a man had justifiable reason to hate people and think that God had let him down, it was Joseph. He was betrayed by his brothers and sold into slavery, lied about by Potiphar's wife and ended up in prison, and forgotten by Pharaoh's baker when assurances to the contrary had been given.

Years after this drama began, God promoted Joseph to the second highest-ranking individual in all of Egypt. God used Joseph in that position to steward the plan that would keep countless people—including Joseph's own brothers—from starvation. Joseph said to his brothers, "Don't you see, you planned evil against me but God used those same plans for my good..." (Genesis 50:20). The NCV reads, "You meant to hurt me, but God turned your evil into good to save the lives of many people, which is being done." The Apostle Paul experienced the same kind of divine working in the midst of great trials. He said, "I want to report to you, friends, that my imprisonment here has had the opposite of its intended effect. Instead of being squelched, the Message has actually prospered" (Philippians 1:12, MSG).

It's important to note that it's not really the trials themselves that bring blessings, but it's what faithful people do in the midst of trials—their trust, their perseverance, and their clinging to God regardless of adverse circumstances—that produces benefits. That's what God uses to bring good out of bad situations.

We need to remember that no temptation, test, or trial we face ever takes God by surprise. God is able to give us all the wisdom and grace necessary to successfully make it through every storm. Before Peter denied Jesus, Jesus told him, "Simon, Simon, Satan has asked to sift each of you like wheat. But I have pleaded in prayer for you, Simon, that your faith should not fail. So when you have repented and turned to me again, strengthen your brothers" (Luke 22:31-32, NLT). Jesus didn't send Peter this problem, but He knew it was coming and prayed for Peter.

Jesus even knew that Peter was going to stumble, and He instructed Peter on what to do after he turned his heart back toward God. Did Peter go through pain in the process? Certainly. When Peter denied Jesus for the third time, we read, "At that moment the Lord turned and looked at Peter. Suddenly, the Lord's words flashed through Peter's mind: 'Before the rooster crows tomorrow morning, you will deny three times that you even know me.' And Peter left the courtyard, weeping bitterly" (Luke 22:61-62, NLT). Despite the consequence of pain, Peter experienced beautiful restoration and a reiteration and clarification of his calling from Jesus (see John 21:15-19). Peter's failure did not short-circuit God's plan for his life, and he went on to do great things for God.

If we get bruised and battered during a storm—whether it be a storm of our own making or one beyond our control—God is there to redeem and restore. Storms may seem to knock us off course, but God can put us back on His path for our life.

Finding Shelter From the Storm

Christians cannot live a problem-free life. Jesus forewarned of persecutions believers would face. There will be inevitable problems that come from living in a fallen world (your tire goes flat; your roof springs a leak), with fallen people (someone loses her temper with you or gossips about you). There might even be storms sent by Satan or created by those he influences. But there are also problems we can avoid. Some we can avoid or minimize just by using wisdom. (Don't spend more than you earn. Wear a seat belt. Work hard on the job.) And we can alleviate some storms through a combination of spiritual and natural attention. For example, we can trust God for physical healing while eating healthy and exercising, and if necessary, go to the doctor for help. Finally, we can avoid some suffering by simply appropriating through faith the blessings—such as salvation—that God has made available to us through Jesus our substitute.

In the middle of a storm, we might wish that we had a storm shelter in the backyard where we could hide out until the storm passes. Just like the many who have survived tornados by escaping to the basement and the countless people who have evacuated to local shelters when hurricanes threatened their home, we long for that safe place where we can wait out the storm. We can build storm shelters for tornados and hurricanes, but there's no place on a map to hide from the storms of life. We can't just sit in our house until it "blows over." But we do have a refuge where we can run, someone we can turn to while the storm rages. We can say with David "I would hurry to my place of shelter, far from the tempest and the storm" (Psalm 55:8, NIV), and, "I long to…take refuge in the shelter of your wings" (Psalm 61:4, NIV). The Bible promises us that "Whoever dwells in the shelter of the Most High will rest in the shadow of the Almighty (Psalm 91:1, NIV).

You and I will face adversity in life. We know that from Scripture. But we also know that God is faithful and that He is committed to seeing us through. May we say with David of old, "For this God is our God for ever and ever: he will be our guide even unto death" (Psalm 48:14, KJV). Regardless of the kind of storm we are facing, God is with us, providing the same grace He gave to the Apostle Paul—grace that is sufficient for us. There is help from Heaven when all hell breaks loose, and I encourage you to let God help you navigate the storms of life and guide you safely to the other side.

Concluding Thought: The Bible addresses different types of suffering, and different principles apply accordingly. Peter said, "...let those who suffer according to the will of God commit their souls to Him in doing good, as to a faithful Creator" (1 Peter 4:19). If there is a suffering that is according to the will of God, it stands to reason that there is a suffering that is not according to the will of God. May God give us the wisdom to know the difference, and the grace to persevere through life's necessary challenges.

Questions for Reflection and Discussion

1. Have you ever blamed God for something you were going through only to realize later that God wasn't the one causing the problems? What changed in your thinking?
2. Have you ever known people who felt like God was behind the problems in their life? Were you able to share anything with them that helped them look at the situation differently? If a person was teachable and wanted your input, what would you share with him to help him understand that God is for him and not against him?
3. Review Jesus' teaching about the people that Pilate murdered and the people who died when the tower of Siloam fell (Luke 13:1-5). Why do you think Jesus responded the way He did and did not more specifically address the reason those people had died?
4. Peter taught extensively about the issue of suffering in his first epistle. Review his remarks (1 Peter 2:19-23; 3:14-17; 4:1-5,12-

16, 19; 5:8-10) and summarize his key thoughts in your own words.

5. How is it that two people can go through similar situations and one comes out bitter and the other person comes out better? Have you grown spiritually while enduring a negative situation? Have you drawn closer to God during a storm? How did you experience this kind of growth in the middle of hard times?
6. How successful have you been at trusting the Lord with all your heart and not leaning to your own understanding? Do you find this admonition in Proverbs 3:5 easy or challenging? Have you been able to trust God even when you haven't been able to understand everything in life?

Appendix

Scriptures for the Storms

For thousands of years, people have found great peace, encouragement, and hope through Scripture. The compilation of passages in this appendix is designed to strengthen your faith as you pass through the storms of life.

> But Moses told the people, "Don't be afraid. Just stand still and watch the LORD rescue you today. The Egyptians you see today will never be seen again."
>
> Exodus 14:13 (NLT)

> This is my command—be strong and courageous! Do not be afraid or discouraged. For the LORD your God is with you wherever you go.
>
> Joshua 1:9 (NLT)

> Thus says the LORD to you: "Do not be afraid nor dismayed because of this great multitude, for the battle is not yours, but God's. You will not need to fight in this battle. Position yourselves, stand still and see the salvation of the LORD, who is with you, O Judah and Jerusalem!" Do not fear or be dismayed; tomorrow go out against them, for the LORD is with you.
>
> 2 Chronicles 20:15,17

> The ropes of death entangled me;
> floods of destruction swept over me.
> The grave wrapped its ropes around me;

death laid a trap in my path.
But in my distress I cried out to the Lord;
yes, I prayed to my God for help.
He heard me from his sanctuary;
my cry to him reached his ears.
He reached down from heaven and rescued me;
he drew me out of deep waters.
He rescued me from my powerful enemies,
from those who hated me and were too strong for me.
They attacked me at a moment when I was in distress,
but the Lord supported me.
He led me to a place of safety;
he rescued me because he delights in me.
You light a lamp for me.
The Lord, my God, lights up my darkness.
In your strength I can crush an army;
with my God I can scale any wall.
God's way is perfect.
All the Lord's promises prove true.
He is a shield for all who look to him for protection.
You have given me your shield of victory.
Your right hand supports me;
your help has made me great.

Psalm 18:4-6; 16-19; 28-30; 35 (NLT)

The Lord is my light and my salvation;
Whom shall I fear?
The Lord is the strength of my life;
Of whom shall I be afraid?

When the wicked came against me
To eat up my flesh,
My enemies and foes,
They stumbled and fell.
Though an army may encamp against me,
My heart shall not fear;
Though war may rise against me,
In this I will be confident.
One thing I have desired of the Lord,
That will I seek:
That I may dwell in the house of the Lord
All the days of my life,
To behold the beauty of the Lord,
And to inquire in His temple.
For in the time of trouble
He shall hide me in His pavilion; In the secret place of His tabernacle
He shall hide me;
He shall set me high upon a rock.

Psalm 27:1-5

The Lord is my Strength and my [impenetrable] Shield; my heart trusts in, relies on, and confidently leans on Him, and I am helped; therefore my heart greatly rejoices, and with my song will I praise Him.

Psalm 28:7 (AMP)

You are my hiding place;
You shall preserve me from trouble;
You shall surround me with songs of deliverance.

Psalm 32:7

The Lord hears his people when they call to him for help.
He rescues them from all their troubles.
The Lord is close to the brokenhearted;
he rescues those whose spirits are crushed.
The righteous person faces many troubles,
but the Lord comes to the rescue each time.

Psalm 34:17-19 (NLT)

The LORD rescues the godly;
he is their fortress in times of trouble.

Psalm 37:39 (NLT)

God is our refuge and strength,
A very present help in trouble.
Therefore we will not fear,
Even though the earth be removed,
And though the mountains be carried into the midst of the sea;
Though its waters roar and be troubled,
Though the mountains shake with its swelling. *Selah*
There is a river whose streams shall make glad the city of God,
The holy place of the tabernacle of the Most High.
God is in the midst of her, she shall not be moved;
God shall help her, just at the break of dawn.
Be still, and know that I am God;
I will be exalted among the nations,
I will be exalted in the earth!

Psalm 46:1-5,10

Cast your burden upon the Lord and He will sustain you;
He will never allow the righteous to be shaken.

Psalm 55:22 (NASB)

Have mercy on me, O God, have mercy!
I look to you for protection.
I will hide beneath the shadow of your wings
until the danger passes by.
I cry out to God Most High,
to God who will fulfill his purpose for me.
He will send help from heaven to rescue me.

Psalm 57:1-3 (NLT)

O God, listen to my cry!
Hear my prayer!
From the ends of the earth,
I cry to you for help
when my heart is overwhelmed.
Lead me to the towering rock of safety,
for you are my safe refuge,
a fortress where my enemies cannot reach me.
Let me live forever in your sanctuary,
safe beneath the shelter of your wings!

Psalm 61:1-4 (NLT)

Be my strong refuge,
To which I may resort continually;
You have given the commandment to save me,
For You are my rock and my fortress.

Psalm 71:3

Those who live in the shelter of the Most High
will find rest in the shadow of the Almighty.
This I declare about the Lord:
He alone is my refuge, my place of safety;
he is my God, and I trust him.
For he will rescue you from every trap
and protect you from deadly disease.
He will cover you with his feathers.
He will shelter you with his wings.
His faithful promises are your armor and protection.

Psalm 91:1-4 (NLT)

In the multitude of my anxieties within me,
Your comforts delight my soul.

Psalm 94:19

Unless the Lord had helped me,
I would soon have settled in the silence of the grave.
I cried out, "I am slipping!"
but your unfailing love, O Lord, supported me.
When doubts filled my mind,
your comfort gave me renewed hope and cheer.

Psalm 94:17-19 (NLT)

Light shines in the darkness for the godly.
They are generous, compassionate, and righteous.
Such people will not be overcome by evil...

They do not fear bad news;
they confidently trust the Lord to care for them.
They are confident and fearless
and can face their foes triumphantly.

Psalm 112:4,6-8 (NLT)

Surely I have calmed and quieted my soul,
Like a weaned child with his mother;
Like a weaned child is my soul within me.

Psalm 131:2

Though I walk in the midst of trouble, You will revive me;
You will stretch out Your hand
Against the wrath of my enemies,
And Your right hand will save me.
The Lord will perfect that which concerns me;
Your mercy, O Lord, endures forever;
Do not forsake the works of Your hands.

Psalm 138:7-8

Trust God from the bottom of your heart;
don't try to figure out everything on your own.

Proverbs 3:5 (MSG)

The name of the Lord is a strong tower;
The righteous run to it and are safe.

Proverbs 18:10

You will keep in perfect peace
all who trust in you,

all whose thoughts are fixed on you!
Trust in the Lord always,
the Lord God is the eternal Rock.

Isaiah 26:3-4 (NLT)

...You are my servant.
For I have chosen you
and will not throw you away.
Don't be afraid, for I am with you.
Don't be discouraged, for I am your God.
I will strengthen you and help you.
I will hold you up with my victorious right hand.

Isaiah 41:9-10 (NLT)

For the mountains may move
and the hills disappear,
but even then my faithful love for you will remain.
My covenant of blessing will never be broken,"
says the Lord, who has mercy on you.
Your enemies will stay far away.
You will live in peace,
and terror will not come near.
But in that coming day
no weapon turned against you will succeed.
You will silence every voice
raised up to accuse you.
These benefits are enjoyed by the servants of the Lord;
their vindication will come from me.
I, the Lord, have spoken!

Isaiah 54:10,14,17 (NLT)

In all their troubles,
he was troubled, too.
He didn't send someone else to help them.
He did it himself, in person.
Out of his own love and pity
he redeemed them.
He rescued them and carried them along
for a long, long time.

Isaiah 63:9 (MSG)

"For I know the plans I have for you," says the Lord. "They are plans for good and not for disaster, to give you a future and a hope."

Jeremiah 29:11 (NLT)

Behold, I give you the authority to trample on serpents and scorpions, and over all the power of the enemy, and nothing shall by any means hurt you.

Luke 10:19

Peace I leave with you, My peace I give to you; not as the world gives do I give to you. Let not your heart be troubled, neither let it be afraid.

John 14:27

I have told you these things, so that in Me you may have [perfect] peace and confidence. In the world you have tribulation and trials and distress and frustration; but be of good cheer [take courage; be confident, certain, undaunted]! For I have overcome the world. [I have deprived it of power to harm you and have conquered it for you.]

John 16:33 (AMP)

...we confidently and joyfully look forward to sharing God's glory. We can rejoice, too, when we run into problems and trials, for we know that they help us develop endurance. And endurance develops strength of character, and character strengthens our confident hope of salvation. And this hope will not lead to disappointment. For we know how dearly God loves us, because he has given us the Holy Spirit to fill our hearts with his love.

Romans 5:2-5 (NLT)

We know that in everything God works for good with those who love him, who are called according to his purpose.

Romans 8:28 (RSV)

No, despite all these things, overwhelming victory is ours through Christ, who loved us.

And I am convinced that nothing can ever separate us from God's love. Neither death nor life, neither angels nor demons, neither our fears for today nor our worries about tomorrow—not even the powers of hell can separate us from God's love. No power in the sky above or in the earth below—indeed, nothing in all creation will ever be able to separate us from the love of God that is revealed in Christ Jesus our Lord.

Romans 8:37-39 (NLT)

Be joyful in hope, patient in affliction, faithful in prayer.

Romans 12:12 (NIV)

I pray that God, the source of hope, will fill you completely with joy and peace because you trust in him. Then you will overflow with confident hope through the power of the Holy Spirit.

Romans 15:13 (NLT)

Every test that you have experienced is the kind that normally comes to people. But God keeps his promise, and he will not allow you to be tested beyond your power to remain firm; at the time you are put to test, he will give you the strength to endure it, and so provide you with a way out.

1 Corinthians 10:13 (GNB)

All praise to the God and Father of our Master, Jesus the Messiah! Father of all mercy! God of all healing counsel! He comes alongside us when we go through hard times, and before you know it, he brings us alongside someone else who is going through hard times so that we can be there for that person just as God was there for us.

2 Corinthians 1:3-4 (MSG)

In the Messiah, in Christ, God leads us from place to place in one perpetual victory parade. Through us, he brings knowledge of Christ. Everywhere we go, people breathe in the exquisite fragrance.

2 Corinthians 2:14 (MSG)

Therefore we do not lose heart. Even though our outward man is perishing, yet the inward man is being renewed day by day. For our light affliction, which is but for a moment, is working for us a far more exceeding and eternal weight of glory, while we do not look at the things which are seen, but at the things which are not seen.

For the things which are seen are temporary, but the things which are not seen are eternal.

2 Corinthians 4:16-18

He said to me, "My grace is sufficient for you, for My strength is made perfect in weakness." Therefore most gladly I will rather boast in my infirmities, that the power of Christ may rest upon me. Therefore I take pleasure in infirmities, in reproaches, in needs, in persecutions, in distresses, for Christ's sake. For when I am weak, then I am strong.

2 Corinthians 12:9-10

Finally, my brethren, be strong in the Lord and in the power of His might. Put on the whole armor of God, that you may be able to stand against the wiles of the devil. For we do not wrestle against flesh and blood, but against principalities, against powers, against the rulers of the darkness of this age, against spiritual hosts of wickedness in the heavenly places. Therefore take up the whole armor of God, that you may be able to withstand in the evil day, and having done all, to stand.

Stand therefore, having girded your waist with truth, having put on the breastplate of righteousness, and having shod your feet with the preparation of the gospel of peace;

above all, taking the shield of faith with which you will be able to quench all the fiery darts of the wicked one. And take the helmet of salvation, and the sword of the Spirit, which is the word of God; praying always with all prayer and supplication in the Spirit.

Ephesians 6:10-18

Don't fret or worry. Instead of worrying, pray. Let petitions and praises shape your worries into prayers, letting God know your concerns. Before you know it, a sense of God's wholeness, everything coming together for good, will come and settle you down. It's wonderful what happens when Christ displaces worry at the center of your life.

Philippians 4:6-7 (MSG)

I have learned how to be content (satisfied to the point where I am not disturbed or disquieted) in whatever state I am.

I know how to be abased and live humbly in straitened circumstances, and I know also how to enjoy plenty and live in abundance. I have learned in any and all circumstances the secret of facing every situation, whether well-fed or going hungry, having a sufficiency and enough to spare or going without and being in want.

I have strength for all things in Christ Who empowers me [I am ready for anything and equal to anything through Him Who infuses inner strength into me; I am self-sufficient in Christ's sufficiency].

Philippians 4:11-13 (AMP)

God has not given us a spirit of fear, but of power and of love and of a sound mind.

2 Timothy 1:7

Do not cast away your confidence, which has great reward. For you have need of endurance, so that after you have done the will of God, you may receive the promise.

Hebrews 10:35-36

...for He [God] Himself has said, I will not in any way fail you nor give you up nor leave you without support. [I will] not, [I will] not, [I will] not in any degree leave you helpless nor forsake nor let [you] down (relax My hold on you)! [Assuredly not!]

So we take comfort and are encouraged and confidently and boldly say, The Lord is my Helper; I will not be seized with alarm [I will not fear or dread or be terrified]. What can man do to me?

Hebrews 13:5-6 (AMP)

Blessed is the man who remains steadfast under trial, for when he has stood the test he will receive the crown of life, which God has promised to those who love him.

James 1:12 (ESV)

Dear brothers and sisters, when troubles come your way, consider it an opportunity for great joy. For you know that when your faith is tested, your endurance has a chance to grow. So let it grow, for when your endurance is fully developed, you will be perfect and complete, needing nothing.

If you need wisdom, ask our generous God, and he will give it to you. He will not rebuke you for asking.

James 1:2-5 (NLT)

You are of God, little children, and have overcome them, because He who is in you is greater than he who is in the world.

1 John 4:4

For every child of God defeats this evil world, and we achieve this victory through our faith.

1 John 5:4 (NLT)

About the Author

Bible teacher and author Tony Cooke has been serving the Body of Christ in various capacities since 1980. His passion for teaching the Bible has taken him to more than forty-five states and to twenty-six nations.

His website (www.tonycooke.org) reaches pastors, missionaries, and other church leaders in more than 190 nations with encouraging and helpful ministerial resources.

Tony was involved in pastoral ministry for more than twenty years, and served as an instructor and the dean of Rhema Bible Training Center. He also served for thirteen years as the director of an International Ministerial Association.

Since 2002, Tony and his wife Lisa have traveled full-time with an assignment of "strengthening churches and leaders."

In addition to being a 1981 graduate of Rhema Bible Training Center, Tony studied Religion at Butler University and received a Bachelor of Science degree in Church Ministries from North Central University.

Tony and his wife, Lisa, reside in Broken Arrow, Oklahoma, and are the parents of two adult children, Laura and Andrew.

Other Teaching Resources by Tony Cooke

hrough the Storm DVD Series
0 Lessons on DVD
leal for Small Group Study with the Book

ife After Death
ediscovering Life After the Loss of a Loved One

Search of Timothy
iscovering and Developing Greatness in Church Staff and Volunteers
Workbook and DVD Series are also available

race
he DNA of God

ualified
erving God with Integrity and Finishing Your Course with Honor

Visit www.tonycooke.org

PRAYER OF SALVATION

God loves you—no matter who you are, no matter what your past. God loves you so much that He gave His one and only begotten Son for you. The Bible tells us that "...whoever believes in Him shall not perish but have eternal life" (John 3:16 NIV). Jesus laid down His life and rose again so that we could spend eternity with Him in heaven and experience His absolute best on earth. If you would like to receive Jesus into your life, say the following prayer out loud and mean it from your heart.

Heavenly Father, I come to You admitting that I am a sinner. Right now, I choose to turn away from sin, and I ask You to cleanse me of all unrighteousness. I believe that Your Son, Jesus, died on the cross to take away my sins. I also believe that He rose again from the dead so that I might be forgiven of my sins and made righteous through faith in Him. I call upon the name of Jesus Christ to be the Savior and Lord of my life. Jesus, I choose to follow You and ask that You fill me with the power of the Holy Spirit. I declare that right now I am a child of God. I am free from sin and full of the righteousness of God. I am saved in Jesus' name. Amen.

If you prayed this prayer to receive Jesus Christ as your Savior for the first time, please contact us on the Web at **www.harrisonhouse.com** to receive a free book.

Or you may write to us at

Harrison House • P.O. Box 35035 • Tulsa, Oklahoma 74153

The Harrison House Vision

Proclaiming the truth and the power

Of the Gospel of Jesus Christ

With excellence;

Challenging Christians to

Live victoriously,

Grow spiritually,

Know God intimately.